SUPREME COURT'S AOR EXAM-DRAFTING

FORMATES OF MORE THAN 25 DRAFTS FOR AOR EXAM PAPER 2 - DRAFTING

JAYPRAKASH BANSILAL SOMANI

To

All the Past & Present Judges of the Supreme Court of India.

Salute to their wisdom.

Salute to their interpretation of Law.

Salute to their elaborative judgement writing.

Supreme Court of India.

Contents

Contents

Contents

Preface

Dear Learned AOR ASPIRENTS Advocates, Advocates ofTrial Court, High Court, Supreme Court and Law Students.

I am very delighted to provide you A Book On **'Supreme Court'sAOR Exam- Drafting'**

In this book you will get more than 25 different drafts of Supreme Court's day to day practice. So Supreme Court's AOR Examination have second paper on Drafting. Some important drafts are as given below.

1. SLP Civil as per Article 136 of the Constitution of India
2. SLP Criminal
3. Counter
4. Different Statutory Appeals
5. Transfer Petitions
6. Writ Petitions
7. Public Interest Litigation
8. Reference by President of India.
9. Election Petition
10. Review Petition
11. Curative Petition
12. Miscellaneous Application & IAs

Thus you will find more than 25 drafting samples in this book.

This book will be helpful to you for breaking AOR Exam and also helpful in regular law practice.

I am thankful to Notion Press to support me to publish & market this book throughout the Country. Thanks to my Juniors, Advocate Colleagues & Insolvency Professional Colleagues to support me in this venture.

Adv. Ekata Verma & Miss. Pooja Rai has helped me a lot to compile this book. I hope this book will add some value addition in the wealth of your legal knowledge. Your positive feedback will boost me to compile/ write further books & negative feedback will improve my skills. Kindly send your valuable feedback by e-mail.

Thanks with Regards,

Jayprakash Bansilal Somani

Advocate, Supreme Court of India

Email: jaysomani64@gmail.com
Web Site: www.jayprakashsomani.com
Call: 9322188701, 8459194576

Acknowledgements

Printed & Published by
Notion Press
No. 8, 3rd Cross Street,
CIT Colony, Mylapore,
Chennai, Tamil Nadu- 600004
Managed by
Jayprakash Somani Advocates & Solicitors
Law Firm for Supreme Court of India
Delhi Office
B- 851, 1st Floor, Shivaji Marg, New Ashok Nagar, Delhi 110096.
Call: 9322188701, 8459194576
Supreme Court Chamber
312, 3rd Floor, M. C. Setalvad Block, In front of 'D' Gate, Bhagwan Das
Road, Supreme Court of India, New Delhi 110001
Contact: 8459194576, 9811011747
www.jayprakashsomani.com
Download our app to get access to our Free Videos, Free Bare Acts,
Free Study Material in Legal as well as International Business Regime.
Android App Link ;-https://clpandrea.page.link/cmSm
Ios APp Link :-https://apps.apple.com/us/app/classplus/id1324522260
Login with org code ;- (qywzji)
Web Link ;-https://qywzji.courses.store/
Opportunity for Lawyers/ Social Workers to get Supreme Court Law
Firm JSAS's authorised centre at District Level.
Kindly Message or Call to: 9322188701
Books are available online in India
1.**Notion Press:**https://notionpress.com/author/jayprakash_somani
2.**Amazon:**https://www.amazon.in/s?k=jayprakash+somani
3.**Flipkart:**https://www.flipkart.com/search?q=Jayprakash%20Somani
Books are available online at International Market
4. **Amazon International:** https://www.amazon.com/
s?k=jayprakash+somani
5. **Amazon United Kingdom:** https://www.amazon.co.uk/
s?k=jayprakash+somani

ACKNOWLEDGEMENTS

6. E-Books/Kindle edition at National & International Level:
https://www.amazon.in/s?k=jaypraksh+somani

CHAPTER ONE

ORDER /RULES IN THE SUPREME COURT RULES, 2013 FOR THE PURPOSE OF DRAFTING

Basically for preparing the syllabus of 2nd paper –Drafting, we have to study the following orders/rules in the Supreme Court Rules, 2013 for the purpose of drafting as :-

- In the matter of Pleadings Generally- **Order XXIX,**
- Plaint- See **Part III** of **Order XXVI,**
- In the matter of Written Statement- **Order XXVIII,**
- In the matter of Appeal under Advocate Act, 1961- **Order XXIII,**
- In the matter of Appeal under Section 23 of Consumer Protection Act, 1986- **Order XXIV,**
- In the matter of Petitions generally- **Order XV,**
- In the matter of Writ Petitions under Article 32 of Constitution of India – **Order XXXVIII,**
- In the matter of Application seeking for transfer under Section 406 of Code of Criminal Procedure- **Order XXXIX,**
- Application seeking for transfer under Article 139(1) of the Constitution- **Order XL,**
- In the matter of Application seeking for Transfer under Article 139A of the Constitution/ Section 25 of the Civil Procedure Code- **Order XLI,**
- In the matter of Election Petition - **Order XLVI,**
- In the matter of Review Petition – **Order XLVII,**

- In the matter of Curative Petition- **Order XLVIII,**
- In the matter of Affidavit – **Order XI,**
- Statement of case – **Order XIX-Rules 35 to 39.**

CHAPTER TWO

SYLLABUS FOR 2ND PAPER I.E. DRAFTING

According to Regulation 4 of "Regulations Regarding Advocates-On-Record Examination" mentioned in 'Supreme Court Rules,2013', the syllabus for Examination of Advocates-On-Record is given, where the syllabus for 2nd paper i.e. Drafting is defined in two parts as :-

1- Petition for Special Leave and Statements of cases etc.,

2- Decrees & Orders and Writs etc.

Where in the word etc. denotes as follows:

- Drafting of Plaints under Original Jurisdiction under Article 131 of Constitution of India,
- Drafting of Petition of Appeals under various Statues and Constitution including under Contempt of Supreme Court,
- Drafting Special Leave Petitions in Civil & Criminal matters,
- Statement of objections in SLPs before grant of Leave to Appeal,
- Miscellaneous Petitions as well as Applications:

A. Misc. Applications like Application for Condonation of Delay, exemptions from surrendering to custody of jail etc.,

B. Application seeking for stay of proceedings in the Court below,

C. Application for granting bail,

D. Application seeking for cancellation of Bail,

E. Application seeking for revocation of Special Leave,

F. Application seeking for intervention,

G. Application seeking for impleadment in the case,

H. Application seeking for filing additional documents,

I. Application seeking for condonation of delay in re-filing the petition/appeal etc.,

J. Application seeking for parole,

- Affidavits i.e. Affidavit in support of the Petition/Appeal as well as Counter Affidavit,
- Statement of case for Petition/respondent,
- Decree and other Forms described under FOURTH SCHEDULE of the Supreme Court rules, 2013 i.e. Form No.1 to Form No.30 as :-

i. Form No.1- Application for the registration of a clerk,
ii. Form No.2- Form of Summons for an order in chambers,
iii. Form No.3- Notice of Appeal from registrar in the Supreme Court of India,
iv. Form No.4- Notice of motion,
v. Form No.5- Form of oath by translator,
vi. Form No.6- Application for production of record,
vii. Form No.7- Notice to the respondent of lodgment of petition of Appeal,
viii. Form No.8- Memorandum of appearance in Person,
ix. Form No.9- Memorandum of Appearance through advocate-on-Record,
x. Form No.10- Certificate to the advocate at the cost of the state,
xi. Form No.11- Notice to Respondent of lodging of Appeal,
xii. Form No.12- Summons for disposal of suit,
xiii. Form No.13- Notice of Appearance,
xiv. Form No.14- Summons for direction,
xv. Form No.15- Notice of payment of money into court,
xvi. Form No.16- Acceptance of sum paid into court,
xvii. Form No.17- Notice to the Attorney-General for India of reference under Article 143 of the Constitution of India,
xviii. Form No.18- Notice to parties of reference under Article 143 of the Constitution of India,
xix. Form No.19- Summons to attend taxation,
xx. Form No.20- Affidavit of Service of summons,
xxi. Form NO.21- Affidavit of service by post,
xxii. Form No.22- Certificate of taxation,
xxiii. Form No.23- Notice for proceedings to Attorney-General for India or Advocate-General of a State,
xxiv. Form No. 24- Writ of commission,

CHAPTER THREE

SUIT UNDER ARTICLE 131 OF THE CONSTITUTION OF INDIA

SUIT UNDER ARTICLE 131 OF THE CONSTITUTION OF INDIA READ WITH RULES UNDER ORDER XXIX OF PART III OF THE SUPREME COURT RULES, 2013
BEFORE THE HON'BLE SUPREME COURT OF INDIA
CIVIL ORIGINAL JURISDICTION

<u>IN THE MATTER OF</u> :-

STATE OF X

THROUGH IT'S SCRETARY ....PLAINTIFF

VERSUS

STATE OF Y

THROUGH IT'S SECRETARY ....DEFENDANT

SUIT UNDER ARTICLE 131 OF THE CONSTITUTION OF INDIA READ WITH RULES UNDER ORDER XXIX OF PART III OF THE SUPREME COURT RULES, 2013

Hon'ble the Chief Justice of India &

His companion Judges of the Supreme Court of India,

The plaintiff above named most respectfully submits as under:-

1. The Plaintiff files the present suit under Article 131 of the Constitution of India read with the Rules under Order XXIX of Part III of the Supreme Court Rules, 2013 seeking relief in terms of prayer against the Defendant.

2. The material and relevant facts giving rise to filing of the present suit may be allowed to be narrated as under:-

(a) ....

(b) ....

(c) ....

(d) ....

(e) ....etc.

3. That the cause of action arose against the defendant State during the ....

4. That the present suit is filed within the period of limitation as it is filed within the prescribed period of limitation commencing from the point of time of failure of the Defendant State to ....

5. That the Plaintiff State is entitled to an amount of Rs.xxxx/- by way of damages/loss caused by the negligence/failure on the part of the Defendant State in ....as the Plaintiff State made huge public investment in ....

6. That the Defendant is liable to perform of its part pursuant to the aforesaid agreement and further suffer a decree of a sum of amount as prayed in terms of prayer made herein below,

7. That this Hon'ble Court has jurisdiction to try the suit under Article 131 of the Constitution of India.

8. That the Plaintiff State has paid a Court Fee of Rs.xxxxx/- on this Plaint/suit as prescribed under Third Schedule of Part IX of the Supreme Court Rules, 2013.

9. That the Plaintiff State is entitled to specific performance of the agreement, the copy of which alongwith other documents, is annexed with the List of Document filed along with this suit.

PRAYER

It is therefore prayed that this Hon'ble Court may be pleased to pass a decree in favour Plaintiff and against the Defendant thereby compelling the Defendant to carry out its part in :-

(a) Specific Performance in terms of the Agreement between the parties; AND;

(b) to pay an amount of Rs.xxxxx/- (RupeesxxxxxxxxxxxxxxxxxxxxOnly) payable to the Plaintiff along with an interest over the said amount @ Rs.yy% p.a. till the amount is paid; AND;

(c) grant any other relief or pass any other order which this Hon'ble Court may deemed fit and proper in the interest of justice, in favour of the

Plaintiff and against the Defendant.

New delhi

Dated:

Plaintiff

By Secretary for the Plaintiff State

Through

Advocate – on Record

Verification:

I, _________________the Secretary for the Plaintiff state do hereby verify that the contents of the Paragraphs 1 to 2 are true and correct to my knowledge derived from the official record of the Plaintiff State maintained at its offices and the contents of the rest paragraphs are believed to be true and correct on the legal advice.

Verified at New delgi on this ____day of ____2023.

Signature

Secretary for the Plaintiff

STATUTORY APPEAL UNDER SECTION 23 OF CONSUMER PROTECTION ACT, 1986

<u>INDEX</u>

Sl.No.	Particulars.		Page Nos.
1.	Office Report on Limitation.	. . . . .	"A"
2.	Check List.	. . . . .	"A1 - A2"
3.	Synopsis, List of Dates & Events.	. . . . .	"B - F"
4.	Copy of the Final Judgment and Order dated _______ passed by the National Consumer Disputes Redressal Commission, New Delhi in Original Petition No. _______.	. . . . .	
5.	Civil Appeal with Affidavit.	. . . . .	
6.	ANNEXURES		
7.			
8.			
9.			
10.			
11.	I.A. NO. _________________ OF 2023 Application for Interim Reliefs.	. . . . .	

IN THE SUPREME COURT OF INDIA
CIVIL APPELLATE JURISDICTION
CIVIL APPEAL NO. _______________ OF 2023

[ARISING FROM THE FINAL JUDGMENT AND ORDER DATED _______ PASSED BY THE NATIONAL CONSUMER DISPUTES REDRESSAL COMMISSION, NEW DELHI IN ORIGINAL PETITION NO. OF]

IN THE MATTER OF

XXXXXX

...APPELLANT

VERSUS

YYYYYYYYYY

...CONTESTING RESPONDENTS

To,

Hon'ble the Chief Justice and his

Hon'ble Companion Justices of the

Hon'ble Supreme Court of India

The humble Appeal of the
Appellant above named –

MOST RESPECTFULLY SHEWETH:

1. This Appeal is a statutory appeal under Section 23 of Consumer Protection Act, 1986 and is directed against Final Order dated __________ passed by the National Consumer Disputes Redressal Commission, New Delhi in Original Petition No. ____________ whereby the Hon'ble National Commission has allowed the complaint and has directed only the Appellant to pay a sum of Rs. ______________ to the complainant.

2. **QUESTION OF LAW**

The Appeal raises the following substantial questions of law, which are of general public importance, for consideration of this Hon'ble Court:

A. Whether the services rendered by Appellant falls within the ambit of word "service" as defined in Section 2(O) of Consumer Protection Act and whether complaint would be maintainable?

B. Whether a Respondent could be termed as a "consumer" in terms of Sec.2(d) of Consumer Protection Act?

C. Whether the impugned judgment is contrary to law laid down by this Hon'ble Court in the judgments in the case of ________________________?

E. Whether the Hon'ble National Commission is correct in law in relying upon the provisions of ___________________?

F. Whether the Hon'ble National Commission erred in law in holding that the Appellant was guilty of negligence and imposing the entire amount of ___________ to Appellant only and not apportioning the amount to other, who had admittedly attended ________________ ?

G. Whether the Hon'ble National Commission was correct in law in accepting the complainant and granting Rs.________/- per month as claimed in the complaint?

H. Whether the amount of Rs. ________given to __________on the ground that during the pendency of the complaint........., is arbitrary, excessive and without any basis?

I. Whether the finding of Hon'ble National Commission that there is deficiency in service and the Appellant has been negligent is perverse and contrary to record, ___________________ ?

J. Whether Hon'ble National Commission erred in law in holding the Appellant solely liable to pay compensation, ________________ ?

L. Whether adverse inference ought to have been drawn by the National Commission for not producing and examining the best available evidence in this case ________________ ?

3. The brief facts of the case are as under:

(a) ....

(b) ....

(c) ....

GROUNDS

4. The Appellant herein craves leave to file the present Appeal on the following amongst other grounds set out herein below without prejudice to one another:

A. Because ....

B. Because...................... (relevant and necessary grounds to the appeal)

P R A Y E R

In the aforesaid facts and circumstances, it is most respectfully prayed that this Hon'ble Court may be pleased to:

(a) Allow the appeal and set aside the order dated _____________ passed by the Hon'ble National Commission in Original Petition No. _____________,AND;

(b) Pass such other order in the facts and circumstances of the case, as this Hon'ble Court may deem fit and proper in the interest of justice.

AND FOR THIS ACT OF KINDNESS, THE APPELLANT AS IN DUTY BOUND SHALL EVER PRAY.

Drawn & Filed by :

Advocate on Record

Place: New Delhi.

Dated : _______________

IN THE SUPREME COURT OF INDIA

CIVIL APPELLATE JURISDICTION

CIVIL APPEAL NO. _______________ OF 2023

IN THE MATTER OF

XXXXXX

...APPELLANT

VERSUS

YYYYYYYYY

...CONTESTING RESPONDENTS

CERTIFICATE IN VIEW OF SUB-CLAUSE 1 RULE 4 ORDER XVI.

Certified that the Civil Appeal is confined only to the pleadings before the Court whose order is challenged and the documents relied upon in those proceedings. No additional facts, documents or grounds have been taken or relied upon in the Civil Appeal. It is further certified that the copies of the documents/annexures attached to the Civil Appeal are necessary to answer the question of law raised in the Petition or to make out grounds urged in the Civil Appeal for the consideration of this Hon'ble Court. This certificate is given on the basis of the instructions given by the Appellant/ person authorised by the Appellant whose affidavit is filed in support of the C.A.

FILED BY :

Advocate on Record

New Delhi

Dated :

IN THE SUPREME COURT OF INDIA

CIVIL APPELLATE JURISDICTION

CIVIL APPEAL NO. _________________ OF 2023

IN THE MATTER OF

XXXXXX

...APPELLANT

VERSUS

YYYYYYYYYY

...CONTESTING RESPONDENTS

A F F I D A V I T

I, _______________s/o _____________________________r/o _________________do hereby solemnly affirm and state as under :

1. That I am the Appellant in the above matter and am conversant with the facts and circumstances of the case. As such I am competent to swear this affidavit.

2. That I have read and understood the contents of para Nos. 1 to ____ on page Nos. __ to __ of the accompanying Civil Appeal filed against the final order dated ____________ passed by the Hon'ble National Consumer Disputes Redressal Commission, New Delhi in Original Petition No. _______________ and state that the facts stated in the Appeal are true to my knowledge and belief.

3. That I have read the accompanying list of dates and events from page B to ____ and say that what is stated therein is true to my knowledge and belief.

4. That I have read the accompanying Application for Interim reliefs and say that what is stated therein is true to my knowledge and belief.

5. The annexures filed along with the Civil Appeal are true copies of their respective originals and formed part of the record of the case.

6. That the Appellant has not filed any other Appeal before this Hon'ble Court against the impugned order of the National Commission.

7. No facts which were not pleaded before the Courts below have been pleaded in the Appeal.

DEPONENT

<u>VERIFICATION</u>:

I, the deponent abovenamed, do hereby verify that the contents of paras 1 to 7 of my above affidavit are true to my knowledge, no part of it is false and nothing material has been concealed therefrom.

Verified at New Delhi on this the ___ day of ___________2023.

IN THE SUPREME COURT OF INDIA

CIVIL APPELLATE JURISDICTION

CIVIL APPEAL NO. ________________ OF 2023

IN THE MATTER OF

XXXXXX ...APPELLANT

VERSUS

YYYYYYYYY ...CONTESTING RESPONDENTS

<u>APPLICATION FOR INTERIM RELIEF</u>

TO,

HON'BLE THE CHIEF JUSTICE AND HIS

HON'BLE COMPANION JUSTICES OF THE

HON'BLE SUPREME COURT OF INDIA

THE HUMBLE APPLICATION OF

THE APPELLANT ABOVE NAMED

MOST RESPECTFULLY SHEWETH:

1. The Appellant have filed the aforesaid Appeal under Section 23 of Consumer Protection Act, 1986 against Final Order dated _____________ passed by the National Consumer Disputes Redressal Commission, New Delhi in Original Petition No. _____________whereby the Hon'ble National Commission has allowed the complaint and has directed only the Appellant to pay a sum of Rs. 8 lacs to the complainant. The Appellant craves leave

of this Hon'ble Court to rely on the same for sake of brevity and to avoid unnecessary repetition. Contentions of the appeal may be read as a part of this application for interim relief.

2. That the Appellant is a ___________________________.

3. It is submitted that the Hon'ble National Commission has allowed the original complaint filed by the complainant, completely overlooking and ignoring the submissions made by the Appellant in the reply and Written Synopsis and has directed only the Appellant to pay the sum of ____________. This is without any basis and has been granted only on humanitarian considerations.

4. The Appellant submit that there is an extremely strong prima facie case in favor of the Appellant and the order of the Hon'ble National Commission is erroneous and untenable. The Hon'ble National Commission has directed the Appellant to pay an amount of to the complainant within 6 weeks from the date of the order. It is submitted that the ______________________________. Grave and irreparable hardship would be caused to the Appellant if the stay of the impugned order is not granted.

7. It is most respectfully submitted that the balance of convenience lies in favour of the Appellant and if stay as prayed for is granted; no harm or prejudice would be caused to the Respondents.

8. It is submitted that in compliance of Section 23 of the Consumer Protection Act, 1986, and Rule 16 of the Consumer Protection Rules, 1987, an amount of Rs. Fifty Thuousand (Rs. 50,000/-) has already been deposited with the Registry of this Hon'ble Court along with the Appeal. The present application has been made bonafide, and in the interest of justice.

P R A Y E R

It is therefore most respectfully prayed that this Hon'ble court may be pleased to:

(i) Grant stay against the Final Order dated ______________ passed by the National Consumer Disputes Redressal Commission, New Delhi in Original Petition No. ____________;

(ii) In the alternative, stay the payment of amount of __________________ as directed by the Hon'ble National Commission pending final disposal of the Appeal;

(iii) Ex-parte ad-interim order in terms of prayer (i) and (ii) above; and

(iv) Pass such other order in the facts and circumstances of the case, as this Hon'ble Court may deem fit and proper in the interest of justice.

AND FOR THIS ACT OF KINDNESS, THE APPELLANT AS IN DUTY BOUND SHALL EVER PRAY.

FILED BY

Advocate on Record

New Delhi

Dated :

CIVIL APPEAL UNDER SECTION 62 OF THE INSOLVENCY AND BANKRUPTCY CODE, 2016

CIVIL APPEAL UNDER SECTION 62 OF THE INSOLVENCY AND BANKRUPTCY CODE, 2016 READ WITH THE PROVISIONS OF ORDER XV OF THE SUPREME COURT RULES, 2013 AGAINST THE FINAL JUDGMENT AND ORDER DATED ....PASSED BY THE HON'BLE NCLAT

IN THE SUPREME COURT OF INDIA

CIVIL APPELLATE JURISDICTION

CIVIL APPEAL NO. ______________ OF 2023

IN THE MATTER OF

XXXXXX ...APPELLANT

VERSUS

YYYYYYYYYY ...CONTESTING RESPONDENTS

CIVIL APPEAL UNDER SECTION 62 OF THE INSOLVENCY AND BANKRUPTCY CODE, 2016 READ WITH THE PROVISIONS OF ORDER XV OF THE SUPREME COURT RULES, 2013 AGAINST THE FINAL JUDGMENT AND ORDER DATED ....PASSED BY THE HON'BLE NCLAT

To,

Hon'ble the Chief Justice and his

Hon'ble Companion Justices of the

Hon'ble Supreme Court of India

The humble Appeal of the
Appellant above named –

MOST RESPECTFULLY SHEWETH:

1. The Appellant above named prefers the present civil appeal under Section 62 of the Insolvency and Bankruptcy Code, 2016 within the prescribed period of limitation of 45 days of the impugned final Judgment and Order of the NCLAT....

2. The facts leading upto filing this appeal are sought to be stated as under:-

(a) ....

(b) ....

(c) ......

3. The appellant filed the present appeal under Section 62 of Insolvency and Bankruptcy Code, 2016 since the following questions of law arising out such order under this Code for the consideration of this Hon'ble Court under appellate jurisdiction of said Section :-

(a) Whether.....................?

(b) Whether.......................?

4. That the Appellant has not filed any other appeal in this Hob'ble Court against the impugned judgment passed by NCLAT.

5. The Appellant prefers the present appeal inter alia on the following grounds :-

GROUNDS

(i) Because the Judgment of the Tribunal is contrary to the law as well as facts of the case and liable t be set aside.

(b) ....

PRAYER

In the aforesaid facts and circumstances, it is most respectfully prayed that this Hon'ble Court may be pleased to:

(a) Allow the appeal in favour of the appellant and set aside the impugned judgment passed by the Hon'ble NCLAT, AND;

(b) Pass such other order in the facts and circumstances of the case, as this Hon'ble Court may deem fit and proper in the interest of justice.

AND FOR THIS ACT OF KINDNESS, THE APPELLANT AS IN DUTY BOUND SHALL EVER PRAY.

Drawn & Filed by :

Advocate on Record

Place: New Delhi.

Dated : _________________

CHAPTER SIX

CRIMINAL APPEAL UNDER SECTION 379 OF Cr.P.C./ SECTION 2 OF [1] OF SUPREME COURT [ENLARGEMENT OF CRIMINAL APPELLATE JURISDICTION] ACT, 1970

CRIMINAL APPEAL UNDER SECTION 379 OF Cr.P.C./ SECTION 2 OF [1] OF SUPREME COURT [ENLARGEMENT OF CRIMINAL APPELLATE JURISDICTION] ACT, 1970 READ WITH ORDER XV AND ORDER XX OF SUPREME COURT RULES, 2013 AND PROVISIONS IN CHAPTOR X OF HAND-BOOK ON PRACTICE AND PROCEDURE/OFFICE PROCEDURE 2017 REGARDING CRIMINAL APPEAL

IN THE SUPREME COURT OF INDIA

CRIMINAL APPELLATE JURISDICTION

CIVIL APPEAL NO. _______________ OF 2023

IN THE MATTER OF

XXXXXX ...APPELLANT

VERSUS

YYYYYYYYYY ...CONTESTING RESPONDENTS

CRIMINAL APPEAL UNDER SECTION 379 OF Cr.P.C./ SECTION 2 OF [1] OF SUPREME COURT [ENLARGEMENT OF CRIMINAL APPELLATE JURISDICTION] ACT, 1970 READ WITH ORDER XV AND ORDER XX OF SUPREME COURT RULES, 2013 AND PROVISIONS IN CHAPTOR X OF HAND-BOOK ON PRACTICE AND PROCEDURE/OFFICE PROCEDURE 2017 REGARDING CRIMINAL APPEAL

To,

Hon'ble the Chief Justice and his

Hon'ble Companion Justices of the

Hon'ble Supreme Court of India

The humble Appeal of the
Appellant above named –

MOST RESPECTFULLY SHEWETH:

1. The Appellant above named prefers the present criminal appeal under section 379 of Cr.p.c./ section 2 of [1] of Supreme Court [Enlargement Of Criminal Appellate Jurisdiction] Act, 1970 read with Order XV and Order XX of Supreme Court Rules, 2013 and provisions in Chapter X of Hand-Book On Practice And Procedure/Office Procedure 2017.

2. The brief facts have been given in Synopsis and the principal steps in the proceedings from the commencement till its conclusion in the Court appealed from are as below :-

(a) ....

(b) ....

(c) ....

3. The appellant filed the present criminal appeal since the following questions of law arising out such order under this Code for the consideration of this Hon'ble Court under appellate jurisdiction of said Section :-

(a) Whether the High Court is justified in reversing the Judgment of acquittal of appellant under Section 386 of Cr.P.C.?

(b) Whether the conviction can be sustained on the testimony of interested witnesses?

(c) Whether Prosecution is required to meet any and every hypothesis put forwarded by the Accused persons?

(d) Whether.....................?

4. The Appellant prefers the present appeal inter alia on the following grounds :-

GROUNDS

(i) Because the Judgment of the Hon'ble High Court is contrary to the law as well as facts of the case and liable to be set aside.

(b) ....

5. That the Appellant has not filed any other appeal in this Hob'ble Court against the impugned judgment except the present appeal.

PRAYER

In the aforesaid facts and circumstances, it is most respectfully prayed that this Hon'ble Court may be pleased to:

(a) Allow the appeal in favour of the appellant and set aside the conviction and sentence of the appellant and the appellant be set at liberty, AND;

(b) Pass such other order in the facts and circumstances of the case, as this Hon'ble Court may deem fit and proper in the interest of justice.

AND FOR THIS ACT OF KINDNESS, THE APPELLANT AS IN DUTY BOUND SHALL EVER PRAY.

Drawn & Filed by :

Advocate on Record

Place: New Delhi.

Dated : _______________

CHAPTER SEVEN

WRIT PETITION UNDER ARTICLE 32 OF THE INDIAN CONSTITUTION

WRIT PETITION UNDER ARTICLE 32 OF THE INDIAN
CONSTITUTION TO PROTECT THE FUNDAMENTAL RIGHT OF THE
PETITIONER GUARANTEED UNDER ARTICLES 14, 16 AND 21 OF
CONSTITUTION OF INDIA
IN THE SUPREME COURT OF INDIA
CIVIL ORIGINAL JURISDICTION
WRIT PETITION (CIVIL) NO.___________ OF 2023
(Under Article 32 of the Constitution of India)

IN THE MATTER OF:-

XXXXXXXXX ...Petitioner

Versus

YYYYYYYYYY ...Respondents

WITH

1. A. No.___________of 2023

Application for exemption from filing Official Translation
(PAPER BOOK)
(FOR INDEX KINDLY SEE INSIDE)
ADVOCATE FOR THE PETITIONER: _____________________

INDEX

SL. NO.	Particulars of Document (Court fees)	Page No. of part to which in belong		Remarks
		Part 1 (Contents of Paper Book)	Part II (Contents of file alone)	
(i)	(ii)	(iii)	(iv)	(v)
1.	Court Fees		Rs.	
2.	Listing Performa	A1-A2	A1-A2	
3.	Cover Page of Paper Book		A-3	

4.	Index of Record of Proceedings		A-4	
5.	Defect List		A-6	
6.	Note Sheet		NS1 to	
7.	Synopsis List of Dates	**B-**		
8.	Writ Petition under Article 32 of the Constitution of India with Affidavit	**1-**		

9.	**APPENDIX:**			
10.	**ANNEXURES:**			
14.	**I.A. NO.______OF 2023:** Application for exemption from filing official translation			
15.	F/M			
16.	V/A			

A1

PROFORMA FOR FIRST LISTING
SECTION:
The case pertains to (Please tick/ check the correct box):-

☐	Central Act: (Title)	**Constitution of India**
☐	Section:	**Article 32**
☐	Central Rule: (Title)	**N.A.**
☐	Rule No(s):	**N.A.**
☐	State Act: (Title)	N.A.
☐	Rule No(s):	**N.A.**
☐	Impugned Interim Order: (Date)	N.A.
☐	Impugned Final Order: (Date)	N.A.
☐	High Court: (Name)	N.A.
☐	Names of Judges:	N.A.
☐	Tribunal/ Authority: (Name)	**Court**

1.	Nature of matter:	[√] **Civil**	[ ]Criminal
2.(a)	Petitioner/ appellant No. 1:		
(b)	e-mail ID:		<u>N.A.</u>
(c)	Mobile phone number:		**N.A**
3.(a)	Respondent No.1:		
(b)	e-mail ID:		**N.A.**
(c)	Mobile phone number:		**N.A.**
4.(a)	Main category classification:		
(b)	Sub classification:		
5.	Not to be listed before:		
6 (a)	Similar disposed of matter with citation, if any & case details:		**No similar disposed of matter**

(b)	Similar pending matter with case details:	**No Similar pending matter.**		
				A2
7.	Criminal Matters:	NO		
(a)	Whether accused/convict has surrendered:	[ ]Yes	[ ]No	
(b)	FIR No.	N.A.	Date:	N.A.
(c)	Police Station:	N.A.		
(d)	Sentence Awarded:	N.A.		
(e)	Period of Sentence Undergone including period of detention/ Custody Undergone	N.A.		
8:	Land Acquisition Matters:			
(a)	Date of Section 4 notification:	N.A.		
(b)	Date of Section 6 notification:	N.A.		
(c)	Date of Section 17 notification:	N.A.		

9.	Tax Matters: State the tax effect:		**N.A.**	
10.	Special Category (first petitioner/appellant only):			
	(i) [X] Senior citizen > 65 years		(ii) [X] SC/ST	
	(iii) [X] Woman/child		(iv) [X] Disabled	
	(v) [X] Legal Aid case		(vi) [X] In custody	
11.	Vehicle Number (in case of Motor Accident Claim matters):		**N.A.**	

Filed by

[ADVOCATE ON RECORD]

RECORD OF PROCEEDINGS

<u>**S.No. DATE OF RECORD OF PROCEEDINGS**</u>

<u>**SYNOPSIS**</u>

That the present Writ Petition under Article 32 of the Constitution of India is being filed to pass an appropriate order/orders and direction/directions in favour of Petitioner to protect the Fundamental Rights guaranteed under Articles 14, 16 and 21 of the Constitution of India.

The important question of law of ....

Special request to Hon'ble Apex Court to consider all grounds given in this Writ petition in the interest of justice.

Case Laws:

1. 2.

<u>**LIST OF DATES**</u>

Hence, the present Writ Petition.

IN THE SUPREME COURT OF INDIA

CIVIL ORIGINAL JURISDICTION

WRIT PETITION (CIVIL) NO.__________ OF 2023

(Under Article 32 of the Constitution of India)

<u>IN THE MATTER OF:-</u>

XXXXXXXXXXXX .....Petitioner

Versus

1YYYYYYYYYYYY ...Contesting Respondents

WRIT PETITION UNDER ARTICLE 32 OF THE INDIAN CONSTITUTION TO PROTECT THE FUNDAMENTAL RIGHT OF ThePETITIONER GUARANTEED UNDER ARTICLES 14, 16 AND 21 OF CONSTITUTION OF INDIA

To,

THE Hon'bleCHIEF JUSTICE OF INDIA

AND HIS COMPANION JUSTICES

OF THE SUPREME COURT OF INDIA

The humble petition of the

PetitionerS above named

MOST RESPECTFULLY SHOWETH:

1. That the Petitioner is filing the present Writ Petition under Article 32 of the Constitution of India in the nature of mandamus to pass an appropriate order/orders and direction/directions in favour of Petitioner to protect the Fundamental Rights guaranteed under Articles 14, 16 and 21 of the Constitution of India.

2. Brief facts of the present writ petition are as under:-

a. That ………

b. ……….

c. ……….

3. It is stated that the Petitioner has faced serious miscarriage of justice because the Review and Curative Petitions filed by the Petitioner were dismissed by this Hon'ble Court.

4. The present Writ Petition under Article 32 of the Constitution is being filed by the Petitioner seeking an appropriate writ, order or direction in the nature of certiorari or such other writ as this Hon'ble Court deems fit, on amongst other the following grounds:-

Grounds

A.   Because ………………

B.   …………………………

C.   …………………………

D.   …………………………

E.   …………………

5. That the Petitioner has not filed any other petition before this Hon'ble Court or any other Court under the same subject matter and with the prayer made herein this petition.

<u>PRAYER</u>

It is, therefore, most respectfully prayed that this Hon'ble Court may kindly be pleased to:-

(a) pass an appropriate orders/directions in favour of Petitioner to protect the Fundamental Rights guaranteed under Articles14, 16 and 21 of the Constitution of India; and/or; or

(b) pass such other order(s) as this Hon'ble Court may deem fit and proper in the facts and circumstances of the present case.

AND FOR THIS ACT OF KINDNESS THE PETITIONERS AS IN DUTY BOUND SHALL EVER PRAY.

DRAWN BY :

(……………………………)

Advocate(Arguing Council)

Drawn on:

Filed on:

FILED BY:

Advocate for the Petitioner

IN THE SUPREME COURT OF INDIA
CIVIL ORIGINAL JURISDICTION
WRIT PETITION (CIVIL) NO. ____________ OF 2023
(Under Article 32 of the Constitution of India)

<u>IN THE MATTER OF:-</u>
XXXXXXXXX

...Petitioner

Versus
YYYYYYYYY

...Respondents

<u>Affidavit</u>

I, ____________, aged about ________ years, Son of ____________________________, resident of ___________________________________, do hereby solemnly affirm and state as under:-

1. That I am the Petitioner in the above noted case and as such I am fully conversant with the facts and circumstances of the case and therefore, I am competent to swear this affidavit.

2. That I have read and understood the contents of Synopsis & List of Dates at Pages B to ___ and Writ Petition as contained in Para 1 to ___ at Pages ___ to ___ and I.A.(s) and state that the facts mentioned therein are true and correct to the best of my knowledge and belief.

3. That the annexures annexed herewith are true and correct copies of their respective originals.

4. That the contents of the above affidavit are true and correct to the best of my knowledge and belief, no part of it is false and nothing material has been concealed therefrom.

<u>VERIFICATION:</u>

Verified at District ______________ on this ____ day of _______,, 2023, that the contents of the above affidavit are true and correct to the best of my knowledge and belief, no part of it is false and nothing material has been concealed therefrom.

IN THE SUPREME COURT OF INDIA
CIVIL ORIGINAL JURISDICTION
I.A.No.__________of 2023
IN
WRIT PETITION (CIVIL) NO.__________ OF 2023

<u>IN THE MATTER OF:-</u>

XXXXXXXX ...Petitioner

Versus

YYYYYYYYYYY ...Respondents

APPLICATION FOR EXEMPTION FROM FILING OFFICIAL TRANSLATION

To,

The Hon'ble Chief Justice of India

And his Companion Judges

Of the Supreme Court of India

The humble petition of the

petitioner above named

MOST RESPECTFULLY SHEWETH:

1. That the Petitioner is filing the present Writ Petition under Article 32 of the Constitution of India in the nature of mandamus to pass an appropriate order/orders and direction/directions in favour of Petitioner to protect the Fundamental Rights guaranteed under Articles 14, 16 and 21 of the Constitution of India.

2. That the detailed facts and circumstances leading to filing of the present application have been set out in the main petition and are not repeated here for the sake of brevity and the same is prayed to be treated as part and parcel of the present application also.

3. That the Annexures P- filed alongwith the accompanying Writ Petition, is originally in vernacular Hindi and the same have been translated by an Advocate well versed in English as well as Hindi.

4. That keeping in view of the urgency of the matter under the facts and circumstances of the case it will be in the interest of justice to exempt the Petitioner from filing the official translation of the above documents.

PRAYER

It is, therefore, most respectfully prayed that this Hon'ble Court may be pleased to:

a) exempt the Petitioner from filing official translation of the Annexures P- ; and

b) pass such order or orders as this Hon'ble Court deems fit and proper in the circumstances of the case.

AND FOR THIS ACT OF KINDNESS THE HUMBLE PETITIONER AS IN DUTY BOUND SHALL EVER.

DRAWN BY :

(_______________) Advocate (Arguing Council)

Drawn on:
Filed on:

FILED BY:

____

Advocate for the Petitioner

REQUEST / APPLICATION UNDER SECTION 11(6) OF THE ARBITRATION AND CONCILIATION ACT, 1996 FOR APPOINTMENT OF ARBITRATORS

IN THE SUPREME COURT OF INDIA

ARBITRATION APPLICATION NO. _________________________ OF 2023

IN THE MATTER OF:

XXXXXX ...Requestors/Applicants

Versus

YYYYYYYY ... Respondent

INDEX

Sl.No. Particulars Page Nos.

1. List of Dates and Events

2. Request/Application under Section 11(6) of the Arbitration and Conciliation Act,

1996 for appointment of arbitrators along with Affidavit.

3. ANNEXURES

Advocates for the Requestors/Applicants : ___________

SYNOPSIS & LIST OF DATES & EVENTS

IN THE SUPREME COURT OF INDIA

ARBITRATION APPLICATION NO. OF 2023

[THE ARBITRATION AND CONCILIATION ACT, 1996 AND THE APPOINTMENT OF AN ARBITRATOR ON BEHALF OF THE RESPONDENT UNDER SECTION 11(6) OF THE ARBITRATION AND CONCILIATION ACT, 1996.]

IN THE MATTER OF:

Xxxxxxxxxx.......Requestors/Applicants

Versus

YYYYYYYYY .....Respondent

REQUEST/APPLICATION TO THE HON'BLE CHIEF JUSTICE OF INDIA UNDER SECTION 11(6) OF THE ARBITRATION AND CONCILIATION ACT, 1996 FOR APPOINTMENT OF ARBITRATORS.

THE HUMBLE REQUEST OF THE REQUESTOR/APPLICANT ABOVE-NAMED:

MOST RESPECTFULLY SHEWETH:

1.That this request to the Hon'ble Chief Justice of India is made under Section 11 (6) of the Arbitration and Conciliation Act, 1996 read with under the Scheme framed by the Supreme Court of India for Appointment of Arbitrators by the Chief Justice of India Scheme, 1996.

2. That the Respondent is a company under the Companies Act, set up with equal equity participation between the Government of India and the Government of National Capital Territory of Delhi for implementation and subsequent operation of Delhi MRTS (Mass Rapid Transit System).

3. The present request pertains to five disputes, which have been raised by the Requestors before the Respondents and, which have been rejected by the Respondents. As more particularly enumerated hereafter efforts for conciliation between the contracting parties proved ineffectual and failed, the Requestors sent the Respondents a proposal to resolve outstanding disputes failing which, the Respondent was asked to treat their letter dated 28th September 2006 (Annexure J) as notice of Arbitration in line with General Conditions of Contract (hereinafter GCC) clause 20.9 quoted below, Clause 20.9 of the GCC requires the Employer/Respondent to maintain a panel of Engineers with requisite qualifications and professional experience. For disputes beyond the claim limit of Rs 1.5 million, the disputes were to be decided by 3 Arbitrators. Further, from this panel, the Employer was to make out a list of five Engineers and the contractor and the Employer were to choose one each and the two so chosen were to choose the third arbitrator from the said list who was to act as presiding arbitrator.

4. Despite notice of arbitration dated 28th September 2006 given by the Requestors, the Employer has not maintained any panel of Engineers nor furnished to the Requestors any list of five Engineers there from or otherwise. More than 30 days have elapsed. As such under Section 11 (6) of the Act, cause of action has arisen in favour of the Requestors for approaching the Hon'ble Chief Justice of India (this being an International Commercial arbitration) to take necessary measures as required by law. On a previous occasion also in a claim arising out of the same contract between the same parties and involving the same/similar issue, in Arbitration Petition No 11 of 2004 the Requestors had approached the Hon'ble Chief Justice of India under Section 11(6). In the said application, Justice S. B. Sinha as nominee of the Hon'ble Chief Justice of India, as agreed by the parties, appointed one arbitrator being the nominee of the Requestors, the second arbitrator being the nominee of the Respondents. A former Chief Justice of India was appointed as the Presiding Arbitrator by the nominee of the Hon'ble Chief Justice of India. It is requested that a like procedure be adopted for appointment in the instant case. A copy of the order dated 12th October 2004 is annexed hereto and marked as Annexure A.

5. The facts with respect to the present application are enumerated hereafter. The present claims relates in brief to the following:-

(a) Claims of the requestors to be compensated from financial loss suffered due to orders of this Hon'ble Court banning mining activities within 5Km of Delhi and also in the entire Aravali Hills

(b) Claims of the requestors for being compensated due to subsequent legislation increasing Excise duty on steel, cement and diesel.

(c) Claim of the requestor for being compensated due to subsequent legislation increasing service tax.

(d) Claim of the requestor with respect to wrongful deduction by the respondent of custom duty.

(e) Claim for reimbursement of Delhi Sales Tax

6. Requestor/Applicant No. 1 is a company duly incorporated and registered under the laws of Japan. Requestor/Applicant No.2 is a company duly incorporated and registered under the laws of Sweden. Requestor/Applicant No.3 is a company duly incorporated and registered under the Indian Companies Act 1956, and Requestor/Applicant No. 4 is company duly incorporated and registered under the laws of Japan. The addresses of the parties to the present application are given in the title to the present request/application.

7. The four Requestors/Applicants entered into a joint venture for the purpose of participating in the bid and in the event of the bid being accepted, for performance of contract MC1A for Delhi Metro Corridor Phase – I. Contract MC1A was a tender floated by the Respondent for design, construction, equipping, testing and commissioning of four underground stations, including approach tracks between Vishwa Vidyalaya to ISBT. The Requestors/ Applicants 1 to 4 are referred to hereafter as Requestors/ Contractor.

8. The Requestors were the successful bidder for Design and Construct Contract MC1A which was awarded to them on 21.5.2001. A copy of the said Contract Agreement MC1A dated 21.5.2001 is annexed herewith and marked as Annexure-"B".

9. The Arbitration Clause is contained in Clause 20 of the General Conditions of Contract (GCC) and forms a part of the Contract Agreement. Under the Contract Clause 20.5, disputes have to be settled by a two stage process, first by Conciliation and in the event it fails, by arbitration under the Arbitration and Conciliation Act, 1996. A certified copy of the relevant Arbitration Agreement Clause 20 is annexed herewith and marked as Annexure-"C". The relevant part of the said Clause being Clause 20.9 reads as follows:

10. Upon failure of the respondent to act in accordance with procedure for appointment agreed upon in Clause 20.9 (as more particularly mentioned hereinafter), the agreement between the parties does not provide "other means for securing the appointment". The Requestor has no other remedy than to move this application.

11. The brief facts necessary for consideration of the present application are as follows:-

(A) ....

(B) ....

(C) ....

[D] Alternatively, this Hon'ble Court may permit the requestors to appoint one arbitrator and this Court may appoint the second arbitrator for the respondent as also the presiding arbitrator. The disputes between the parties are legal in nature and it is submitted it is appropriate that the Presiding Arbitrator preferably be a retired Judge of this Hon'ble Court.

[E] Since this Contract has been completed and the issues raised in the present arbitration are the only issues, which presently remain to be resolved between the parties, it is prayed that the Arbitration Panel be directed to decide the dispute within a period of 4 months.

P R A Y E R

The Requestor therefore, most respectfully prays that

this Hon'ble Court may be pleased to:

(a) appoint ________________ (Retired Chief Engineer, CPWD) as nominee of the Requestor, appoint second arbitrator as nominated by the Respondent and appoint any former Judge of this Hon'ble Court as the presiding arbitrator;

(b) in the alternative, if no name is suggested by the Respondent, this Hon'ble Court may appoint ________________as nominee of the Requestor, appoint an engineer or former Judge of this Hon'ble Court as the second arbitrator and also appoint a former Judge of this Hon'ble Court as the presiding arbitrator; and

(c) pass such other and further order or orders as this Hon'ble Court may deem fit and proper in the facts and circumstances of the case.

Filed by:

____

Counsel for the Requestors

Drawn on:

Place: New Delhi:

Dated:

❧❧❧

CHAPTER NINE

PETITION UNDER SECTION 11(9) OF THE ARBITRATION AND CONCILIATION ACT, 1996

IN THE SUPREME COURT OF INDIA
(CIVIL ORIGINAL JURISDICTION)
ARBITRATION PETITION NO. ___________ OF 2023

<u>IN THE MATTER OF:</u>

XXXXXXX ...Petitioner

VERSUS

YYYYYYY ...Respondent

PETITION UNDER SECTION 11(9) OF THE ARBITRATION AND CONCILIATION ACT, 1996.

TO

THE HON'BLE CHIEF JUSTICE OF INDIA
AND HIS COMPANION JUSTICES OF THE
SURPEME COURT OF INDIA

THE HUMBLE PETITION OF THE
PETITIONER ABOVE NAMED

<u>MOST RESPECTFULLY SHEWETH:</u>

1. The present petition is being filed by the petitioners under Section 11 (9) of the Arbitration and conciliation Act, 1996 (hereinafter referred to as the 'said Act') as the Respondents have, inspite of receipt of the notice for appointment of Arbitrator and in spite of repeated requests being made by the Petitioner, failed to appoint their Arbitrator in terms of Clause 7 of the

Agreement dated 20.02.2002.

2. The Petitioner is a company incorporated under the provisions of the Indian Company's Act, 1956 and has its Registered Office at No. 14, N.R. Towers, BTM Layout 1 Stage, Bangalore 560 068. The Petitioner is engaged in the business of ECRM Services and Call Centre facilities providing information technology related through its service providers.

3. The Respondent is a company incorporated under the Canadian Laws having its registered office at 111B, ST. Catherine West 502, Montreal (Quebec), Canada, H3B-1HS and is engaged in the business of Call Centre and Call Centre related technologies.

4. The facts that give rise to the present petition are briefly mentioned as hereunder:-

a) ....

b) ....

c)................

5. The respondents in pursuance to the said clause have invoked the Arbitration Clause vide a Legal Notice dated .... A true copy of the letters, the Legal Notice and the Postal Acknowledgement for having received the aforesaid Notice is collectively annexed hereto and marked as <u>ANNEXURE</u> .....

6. However the Respondent inspite of receipt of notice for appointment of Arbitrator and in spite of repeated requests being made by the Petitioner, failed to appoint their Arbitrator in terms of Clause 7 of the Agreement dated 20.02.2002. In view of the above the Petitioner respectfully submits that the Hon'ble Chief Justice of India and/or any person or Institution designated by the Hon'ble Chief Justice may be pleased to appoint the aforesaid Arbitrator as the sole Arbitrator to adjudicate the dispute of the parties.

7. The Petitioner states that since the Respondent is a company incorporated in a country outside India and carries on business outside India and the Petitioner being a company registered under the Indian Company's Act having its registered office in India, the Arbitration Clause would make it an 'International Commercial Arbitration' as defined under Section 2 (1)(f) of the Act, 1996.

8. Since the Arbitration contemplated in the present proceedings is an International Commercial Arbitration, this Hon'ble Court has jurisdiction to entertain the same and grant the reliefs as prayed for.

9. The Petitioner submits that they have not filed any other petition before any other Court in India or before this Hon'ble Court seeking the same relief against the Respondents. No such petition is pending at present. No other reliefs beyond the ambit of the Agreement has been claimed in this Petition.

In the above facts and circumstance, it is most respectfully prayed that this Hon'ble Court may graciously be pleased to :-

PRAYER

a. Grant the appointment of the sole Arbitrator Mr. Justice (Retd.) A.A. Halbe, "Prachi Judges Society", Behind HDFC Bank, Juhu Versova Link Road, Andheri West, Mumbai # 400 053 under Section 11(6) (A) AND Section 11 (9) of the Arbitration and Conciliation Act, 1996, and

b. Grant cost of the Petitioner and/or.

c. pass any other order or further orders as may be deemed fit and proper in the facts and circumstances of the case.

ADVOCATE FOR THE PETITIONER

SPECIAL LEAVE PETITION (CIVIL) (UNDER ARTICLE 136 OF THE CONSTITUTION OF INDIA READ WITH ORDER XVI RULE 4 (1)(A) OF THE SUPREME COURT RULES, 2013

INDEX

IN THE SUPREME COURT OF INDIA
(Order XVI Rule 4 (1)(a)

CIVIL APPELLATE JURISDICTION
SPECIAL LEAVE PETITION
(Under Article 136 of the Constitution of India)
SPECIAL LEAVE PETITION (CIVIL) NO.__________ OF 2023
WITH PRAYER FOR INTERIM RELIEFS

(Arising out of the final Judgment and Order dated ____________ passed by the Hon'ble High Court of Judicature at _________in Writ Petition No. ____________)

1. xxxxxxxxxxxx Petitioner No.1 Petitioner No. 1

AND

YYYYYYYYYYYYY Respondent ContestingRespondent No. 1

To

Hon'ble The Chief Justice of India

And His Hon'ble Companion Justices of

The Hon'ble Supreme Court of India

The humble Petition of the Petitioner above-named :

MOST RESPECTFULLY SHEWETH:

1. The Petitioner is filing the present Petition under Article 136 of the Constitution of India for seeking Special Leave to appeal against the final Judgment and Order dated _____________ passed by the Hon'ble High Court of Judicature at ____________ in Writ Petition No. _____________ whereby the Hon'ble High Court dismissed the Application filed by Petitioner seeking directions from the Hon'ble High Court to enable the Office to take the Bank Guarantee on record, in the interest of justice, since the office had refused to accept the same on the ground that the time of four weeks granted by this Hon'ble Court on _____________ had already elapsed.

2. **QUESTIONS OF LAW:**

The present Special Leave Petition raises the following substantial questions of law and of general/public importance which require the consideration of this Hon'ble Court:

I. Whether the Hon'ble High Court has erred in law in taking a hypertechnical view and dismissing the application for accepting the Bank Guarantee solely on the ground that since the four weeks period granted in order dated ___________ for furnishing the Bank Guarantee had already expired and there was no stay order operating, the application for extending the stay order was "misconceived"?

II. Whether the Hon'ble High Court has committed a serious error in law in ignoring that the Courts in granting interim injunctions have wide discretionary powers and such a hypertechnical approach was unwarranted and unjust in the facts of the present case, namely that the Petitioner had already been granted interim injunction by the very same court on ____________ and that the delay in filing Bank Guarantee was genuine and not on account of any lackadaisical attitude of the Petitioners?

III. Whether the Hon'ble High Court has failed to appreciate that the cause for delay in furnishing Bank Guarantee was a genuine one namely that when the Petitioners approached their usual bankers HDFC Bank with the format of the Bank Guarantee given by the Registry of the High Court, the Petitioner's bank refused to furnish a bank guarantee as per the format since it required the bank guarantee to have an "auto-renewal" clause, and thus, the Petitioner's had to approach another Bank for the Bank Guarantee, which circumstance could not have been reasonably forseen by the Petitioner and was beyond the Petitioner's control?

IV. Whether the Hon'ble High Court ought to have appreciated that the Petitioner through earnest efforts managed to procure a bank guarantee from a bank other than its usual bank and even attempted to furnish the same, but the Registry would not accept it on account of delay, thus, the Petitioners were constrained to move an application/praecipe for the same?

V. Whether the Hon'ble High Court has committed a serious error in law in dismissing the application for extension of interim injunction by ignoring the three settled principles of the law of grant of interim injunction, namely (i) prima facie case, (ii) balance of convenience and (iii) grave and irreparable injury?

VI. Whether the Hon'ble High Court failed to appreciate that no loss or injury was caused to either party on account of the inadvertent delay in filing the Bank Guarantee, and that in any event, the Petitioners were and are ready and willing to furnish the Bank Guarantee?

VII. Whether the Hon'ble High Court failed to appreciate that this was a fit case for grant of interim protection since the Petitioner's were apprehending demolition of their cell sites at the hands of the Respondent-Corporation, and since the High Court itself had even earlier *vide* order dated 25.2.2008 granted such interim protection?

3.DECLARATION IN TERMS OF RULE 4(2):

The Petitioner has not filed any other Petition seeking reliefs to Appeal against the Impugned Judgment and Order.

4.DECLARATION IN TERMS OF RULE 6:

The Annexures P-1 to P- produced along with the SLP are true and correct copies of the pleadings/documents which formed part of the record of the case in the Court below against whose order the leave to appeal is sought for in this petition.

5. GROUNDS:

The present Special Leave to appeal is sought for on the following amongst other grounds which are taken in the alternative and without prejudice to one another:

A. Because the Hon'ble High Court has erred in taking a hypertechnical view and dismissing the application for permission to file Bank Guarnatee belatedly and for extension of interim protection in favour of the Petitioner, solely on the ground that since the four weeks period granted in order dated __________ had already expired and there was no stay order operating, the application for extending the stay order was "misconceived".

B. Because the Hon'ble High Court failed to appreciate that the failure to furnish Bank Guarantee within four weeks was completely inadvertent and was on account of the unexpected refusal of the Petitioner's bank in furnishing the Bank Guarantee. **The Petitioner has not been lackadaisical in complying with the condition imposed in the order dated __________ and in fact procured the format of the Bank Guarantee in time from the High Court Registry and submitted the same well within time to its bank for the purpose of issuing a Bank Guarantee. However, to the utter surprise of the Petitioner, the Petitioner's Bank informed the Petitioner on ________ that it would not be able to issue the Bank Guarantee since the format required the same to contain an "auto-renewal" clause, which clause was not acceptable to the Bank. The Petitioner then had no option but to approach another bank, which it did immediately upon being intimated about the refusal by its usual bank. Therafter, as soon as the Petitioners procured the Bank Guarantee, they immediately rushed to the Registry with the same, but unfortunately, by then the four weeks period granted in order of __________ had expired, and the Bank Guarantee was not accepted by the Registry.**
Thus, through no fault of the Petitioner, on account of this reasonably unforeseeable circumstance of the Petitioner's Bank refusing to issue

Bank Guarantee and consequently the Petitioner having to approach another bank, i.e. SBI, there was delay of only _________ days in procuring the Bank Guarantee.

C. Because the Hon'ble High Court has ignored the settled principles of the law of grant of interim injunction in refusing to extend the interim protection

D. Because the Hon'ble High Court failed to appreciate that no loss or injury was caused to either party on account of the inadvertent delay in filing the Bank Guarantee, and that in any event, the Petitioners were and are ready and willing to furnish the Bank Guarantee. Thus, no harm or prejudice would have been caused to either side if the Hon'ble High Court would have extended the stay protection and allowed the Petitioners to file the correct Bank Guarantee.

E. Because the Hon'ble High Court failed to appreciate that this was a fit case for grant of interim protection since the Petitioner's were apprehending demolition of their cell sites at the hands of the Respondent-Corporation, and since the High Court itself had even earlier *vide* order dated ----------- granted such interim protection, and again on ------------, on C.A. filed by the Petitioner the High Court had taken oral undertaking from the Respondent-Corporation to abide by the order dated ------------------- not to demolish the subject structures of the Petitioners and further directed the Respondent to return to the Petitioners any equipment seized or attached to enable the Petitioners to make the towers which had been rendered un-operational, operational again.

F. Because the Hon'ble High Court has failed to appreciate that a Court deciding on interim injunction has wide discretionary powers and such hypertechnical approach was unwarranted and unjust in the facts of the present case. Even though the stay period of four weeks granted earlier *vide* order ------------- had come to an end, the Hon'ble High Court had full powers to, and in fact ought to have, granted the Petitioner permission to file the rectified Bank Guarantee and directed interim stay against demolition to continue/resume, in view of the fact that the stay had been made conditional only upon furnishing bank guarantee within four weeks which condition the Petitioner was willing to comply with, and it was only due to a bona fide erroneous belief on the part of the Petitioners that there had been some inadvertent delay in filing the same. The High Court failed to appreciate that this was fit case in which the ends of justice would have been met by permitting the Petitioners to furnish the Bank Guarantee and by continuing/resuming the interim injunction.

G. Because the Hon'ble High Court has erred in as much as the Hon'ble High Court has effectively punished the Petitioner for its diligence in moving a formal application for continuation of stay and by taking a hypertechnical approach has refused to extend the interim protection to the Petitioner, which had been granted to it as early as --------------, merely because the Petitioner due to a *bona fide* mistaken belief, could not furnish a Bank Guarantee from a nationalised bank within the four weeks granted *vide* order dated -----------.

(Add grounds as per the necessity of the case)

6. GROUNDS FOR INTERIM RELIEF:

A. In the aforementioned facts and circumstances of the case, it is a fit case for the grant of interim reliefs as prayed for.

B. The Petitioners have a prima facie good case and the balance of convenience lies in their favour.

C. In view of the aforesaid it is a fit case for grant of interim reliefs as prayed for.

7. MAIN PRAYER

It is respectfully submitted in the circumstances that this Hon'ble Court may be pleased to:

(a) grant Special Leave to Appeal to the Petitioners against the final Judgment and Order dated ___________ passed by the Hon'ble High Court of Judicature at ____________ in Writ Petition No. _____________ ;

(b) to pass such further and other orders as may be deemed just and proper in the facts and circumstances of the case.

8. INTERIM RELIEFS:

(a) stay the operation and implementation of the final Judgment and Order dated _______________ passed by the Hon'ble High Court of Judicature at ___________ in Writ Petition No_______________ ;

(b) stay the operation of the demand notices dated _________________ and restrain the Respondents from demolishing the cellular sites of the Petitioner situated in the region of Navi Mumbai;

(c) grant ad interim ex-parte orders in terms of prayers (a) and (b) above; and

(d) pass such other and further order or orders as this Hon'ble Court may deem fit and proper in the facts and circumstances of the case.

FILED BY :

____

Advocates for the Petitioner
Drawn on
Dated :

CHAPTER ELEVEN

SPECIAL LEAVE PETITON (CRIMINAL) UNDER ARTICLE 136 OF THE CONSTITUTION OF INDIA READ WITH ORDER XXI RULE 3(1)(a) OF THE SUPREME COURT RULES, 2013

IN THE SUPREME COURT OF INDIA
[SCR Order XXI Rule 3(1)(a)]
CRIMINAL APPELLATE JURISDICTION
[Under Article 136 of the Constitution of India]
SPECIAL LEAVE PETITION (Crl.) NO.________OF 2023
(WITH PRAYER OF INTERIM RELIEF)
(Arising from the impugned judgment and final order dated
__________ passed by the Hon'ble High Court of ______________ in
Criminal Petition No. ________________)

<u>IN THE MATTER OF</u>:

XXXXXXX ...Petitioner

Versus

YYYYYYY ...Respondent

PAPER BOOK

[FOR INDEX KINDLY SEE INSIDE]
ADVOCATE FOR THE PETITIONER: ________________
(________)

INDEX

SL. NO.	Particulars of Document	Page No. of part to which in belong		Remar ks
		Part 1 (Contents of Paper Book)	Part II (Contents of file alone)	
(i)	(ii)	(iii)	(iv)	(v)
1.	O/R Limitation			
2.	Listing Performa			
3.	Cover Page of Paper Book			
4.	Index of Record of Proceedings			
5.	Limitation Report prepared by the Registry			
6.	Defect List			
7.	Note Sheet			
8.	Synopsis List of Dates	B-		
9.	True copy of the impugned judgment and order dated ________ passed by the Hon'ble High Court in ________ Criminal Petition No. ________.	1-		
10.	Special Leave Petition with affidavit			
11.	Appendix:			
11.	ANNEXURES			

IN THE SUPREME COURT OF INDIA

[SCR Order XXI Rule 3(1)(a)]
CRIMINAL APPELLATE JURISDICTION
[Under Article 136 of the Constitution of India]
SPECIAL LEAVE PETITION (Crl.) NO.________OF 2023
(WITH PRAYER OF INTERIM RELIEF)
(Arising from the impugned judgment and final order dated __________ passed by the Hon'ble High Court of _____________ in Criminal Petition No. ______________)

<u>IN THE MATTER OF</u>:

XXXXXXX ...Petitioner

Versus

YYYYYYY ...Respondent

<u>**OFFICE REPORT ON LIMITATION**</u>

1.The petition is within time.

2. The Petition is not barred by time and there is no delay in filing the same against the order dated 22.02.2023.

3. There is delay of ____ days in re-filing the petition and petition for condonation of __ days delay in re-filing has been filed.

BRANCH OFFICER

NEW DELHI

Dated:

A1

PROFORMA FOR FIRST LISTING
SECTION:
The case pertains to (Please tick/ check the correct box):-

☐	**Central Act: (Title)**	IPC
☐	**Section:**	
☐	**Central Rule: (Title)**	N.A.
☐	**Rule No(s):**	N.A.
☐	**State Act: (Title)**	N.A.
☐	**Rule No(s):**	N.A.
☐	**Impugned Interim Order: (Date)**	N.A.
☐	**Impugned Final Order: (Date)**	
☐	**High Court: (Name)**	
☐	**Names of Judges:**	
☐	**Tribunal/ Authority: (Name)**	Court

1.	Nature of matter:	[] Civil	[√]Criminal
2.(a)	Petitioner/ appellant No. 1:		
(b)	e-mail ID:		<u>N.A.</u>
(c)	Mobile phone number:		N.A.
3.(a)	Respondent No.1:		
(b)	e-mail ID:		<u>N.A.</u>
(c)	Mobile phone number:		N.A.
4.(a)	Main category classification:		14 Criminal matterS
(b)	Sub classification:		1418 Others
5.	Not to be listed before:		N.A.
6 (a)	Similar disposed of matter with citation, if any &case details:		No Similar disposed matter.
(b)	Similar pending matter with case details:		No Similar pending matter. A2
7.	Criminal Matters:		YES
(a)	Whether accused/convict has surrendered:	[√]Yes	[]No

(b)	FIR No.	N.A.	Date:	N.A.
(c)	Police Station:		P.S. BedakamN.A., Kerala	
(d)	Sentence Awarded:	N.A.		
(e)	Period of Sentence Undergone including period of detention/ Custody Undergone	N.A.		
8:	Land Acquisition Matters:			
(a)	Date of Section 4 notification:	N.A.		
(b)	Date of Section 6 notification:	N.A.		
(c)	Date of Section 17 notification:	N.A.		
9.	Tax Matters: State the tax effect:	N.A.		
10.	Special Category (first petitioner/appellant only):			
	(i) [X] Senior citizen >		(ii) [X] SC/ST	
	(iii) [X] Woman/child		(iv) [X] Disabled	
	(v) [X] Legal Aid case		(vi) [X] In custody	
11.	Vehicle Number (in case of Motor Accident Claim matters):	N.A.		

Filed by

[________________]

Advocate for the Petitioner

Registration No.______

Email ID: ___________________

Dated: (M) ________________

Synopsis & List of Dates

IN THE SUPREME COURT OF INDIA

[SCR Order XXII Rule 2(1)]

CRIMINAL APPELLATE JURISDICTION

[Under Article 136 of the Constitution of India]

SPECIAL LEAVE PETITION (Crl.) NO.______OF 2023

(WITH PRAYER OF INTERIM RELIEF)

B E T W E E N: POSITION OF PARTIES

In the IN THEIN THIS
Trial Court High Court COURT
XXXXXXXXXXXX Respondent PetitionerPetitioner
Versus
YYYYYYYYYYYYYY Petitioner Respondent Respondent
To,
THE HON'BLE CHIEF JUSTICE OF INDIA
AND HIS COMPANION JUSTICES
OF THE SUPREME COURT OF INDIA
The humble petition of the Petitioner above named,
<u>**MOST RESPECTFULLY SHOWETH:**</u>

1.That the petitioner is filing the present Special Leave Petition under Article 136 of the Constitution of India against the impugned judgment and final order dated ___________ passed by the Hon'ble High Court of _______________ in Criminal Petition No. __________________, wherein the Hon'ble High Court was pleased to allow the Criminal Petition in Part filed by the Petitioner.

2. QUESTIONS OF LAW:

- The following substantial questions of law arise for consideration of this Hon'ble Court:-WHETHER the Hon'ble High Court ought not to have appreciated the settled position of law with regard to the perjury and suppression of facts & materials as laid by this Hon'ble Court in catena of judgments?
- WHETHER the courts below ought not to have appreciated that the petitioner has rightly approached the Ld. Trial Court by way of filing the Interlocutory Applications under section 91 & 340 of Cr.pc ?
- WHETHER, the impugned order is legally sustainable being passed in contradiction of the relevant statutory provisions of law?
- WHETHER the courts can adopt hard and fast rule while deciding the application under sections 91 & 340 of Cr. PC?
- WHETHER the Hon'ble High Court was correct in not appreciating that Memo filed by the Ld. Counsel of the Respondent?

3.DECLARATION IN TERMS OF RULE 2(2):
The Petitioner states that no other petition seeking leave to appeal has been filed by her against the impugned judgment and order dated _______ passed by the Hon'ble High Court of _________________ in Criminal

Petition No. _______________________.

4.DECLARATION IN TERMS OF RULE 4:

The Annexures P-1 to P-19 produced along with the Special Leave Petition are true copies of the proceedings/ documents which formed part of the records of the case in the case in the court below against whose order the leave to appeal is sought for in this petition.

5. G R O U N D S:

The Special Leave to Appeal is sought for on the following grounds:-

A. Because the Hon'ble High Court have failed to appreciate the reliance precedent held by this Hon'ble Court in the Judgment of ....

B. Because the Hon'ble High Court as well as Ld. Family Court have failed to appreciate the essentials of the section 5 and 11 of Hindu Marriage Act 1955 as According to Section 5(i) of the Hindu Marriage Act 1955

C. Because the Hon'ble High Court as well as Ld. Family Court have failed to appreciate the ....

D. Because the Hon'ble High Court as well the Ld. Family Court have failed to provide the reasonable opportunity to the Petitioner.

E. That the other grounds would be urged at the time of hearing. (can add reasonable and necessary grounds as per the case)

6.GROUNDS FOR INTERIM RELIEF:

A.That the facts and law stated in synopsis & List of Dates and the main SLP may be treated as part and parcel of this paragraph. The same is not being repeated for the sake of brevity.

B. That the Petitioner respectfully submits that in view of the submissions made in the forgoing paragraphs he has a strong prima facie case. If the interim relief is not granted to the Petitioner during the pendency of the present Special Leave Petition, the petitioner shall suffer an irreparable loss and injury.

C. In view of the aforesaid it is a fit case for grant of interim reliefs as prayed for.

D. BECAUSE the Hon'ble High Court had passed the impugned order/ judgment in ignorantium and contrary to the judgment laid by this Hon'ble Court in catena of judgment as quoted above thereby depriving the petitioner from defending its case on merits.

7. MAIN PRAYER:

In the circumstances, it is most respectfully prayed that Your Lordships may graciously be pleased to:

a) grant Special Leave to Appeal against the impugned judgment and final order dated _________ passed by the Hon'ble High Court of ________________ in Criminal Petition No________________; and

b) pass such further, order/s, direction/s as this Hon'ble Court may deem fit in the interest of justice.

8. PRAYER FOR INTERIM RELIEF:

It is most respectfully prayed that this Hon'ble Court may be pleased to:-

a. Stay the proceedings of the Ld. Family Court at ____________ in Crl. Misc.____________ to meet the ends of justice during the pendency of the present Special Leave Petition; and

b. pass such further order/s, direction/s as this Hon'ble Court may deem fit in the interest of justice.

AND FOR THIS ACT OF KINDNESS, THE PETITIONER AS IN DUTY BOUND SHALL EVER PRAY.

Drawn &FILED BY

Drawn On: (________________)

Filed On:Advocate for the Petitioner.

CHAPTER TWELVE

REVIEW PETITION UNDER ORDER XLVII OF THE SUPREME COURT RULES, 2013

IN THE SUPREME COURT OF INDIA
CIVIL APPELLATE JURISDICTION
REVIEW PETITION No. _______ of 2023
IN
SPECIAL LEAVE PETITION (C) NO. ________OF 2023
(Arising from the final Judgment and Order dated ________ passed by
this Hon'ble Court in Special Leave Petition No. _________ of 2023)

BETWEEN:

XXXXX ...Review Petitioners

A N D

YYYYYY ...Respondent

W I T H

I.A. NO. ___________________________ OF 2023

Application for condonation of delay in filing

Review Petition

W I T H

I.A. No. __________________ of 2023

Application For Exemption from Filing Certified Copy of the Impugned

Judgment and order.

(FOR INDEX PLEASE SEE INSIDE)

ADVOCATES FOR THE REVIEW PETITIONERS :

I N D E X

SYNOPSIS & LIST OF DATES AND EVENTS

The present review Petition is being filed against the order dated passed by this Hon'ble Court in Special Leave Petition No. _________ whereby this Hon'ble Court dismissed the said SLP at the admission stage.

The brief facts of the case are as follows:

IN THE SUPREME COURT OF INDIA
CIVIL APPELLATE JURISDICTION

REVIEW PETITION NO._______ 2023

IN

SPECIAL LEAVE PETITION NO. _______ OF 2023

BETWEEN:

XXXXXXXX ......Petitioner

A N D

YYYYYY ... Respondent

PETITION FOR REVIEW OF ORDER DATED ________ PASSED IN SLP NO. _______ OF 2008 UNDER ARTICLE 137 OF THE CONSTITUTION OF INDIA READ WITH ORDER XLVII OF THE SUPREME COURT RULES, 2013.

To

Hon'ble the Chief Justice and His

Hon'ble Companion Justices of the

Hon'ble Supreme Court of India

The humble Petition of the Review Petitioners above named : -

MOST RESPECTFULLY SHOWETH:

1. This is a Petition under Order XLVII 1 of the Supreme Court Rules, 2013 inter alia praying for review of the order dated ________ passed by this Hon'ble Court in Special Leave Petition No. ________ of 2023 by which this Hon'ble Court dismissed the Special Leave Petition filed by the Review Petitioners at the admission stage.

2. The Review Petitioners humbly submit that the order dated ________ is sought to be reviewed on the grounds of errors apparent on the face of record and also in view of this Hon'ble Court not considering that the ....

3. The facts leading to the filing of the present petition are as under: -

(i) ....

(ii) ....

(iii) ....etc.

4. The petitioner begs to submit that inasmuch as the points raised by the petitioner were not considered by this Hon'ble Court, there is an error apparent on the face of the record.

5. The Oetitioner respectfully submits that this Hon'ble Court may be pleased to review the order dated ___________ on the following amongst other grounds which are taken without prejudice to one another.

GROUNDS

A. Because this Hon'ble Court...................(all relevant and necessary grounds as per the case)

PRAYER

In the aforementioned facts, circumstances and submissions, it is most respectfully prayed that this Hon'ble Court may graciously be pleased to:

(a) review the judgment and order dated _______________ passed by this Hon'ble Court in Special Leave Petition No. _______________ of 2023 and thereafter rehear the special Leave Petition and allow the same; and

(b) pass such other and further order(s) as this Hon'ble Court may deem fit and proper in the facts and circumstances of the case.

Filed by

Advocates for the Review Petitioners

New Delhi

Drawn on :

Filed on:

CHAPTER THIRTEEN

CURATIVE PETITION UNDER ORDER XLVIII OF THE SUPREME COURT RULES, 2013

IN THE SUPREME COURT OF INDIA
EXTRAORDINARY CIVIL APPELLATE JURISDICTION
CURATIVE PETITION (CIVIL) NO. OF 2023
IN
REVIEW PETITION NO. _______ OF 2023
IN
CIVIL APPEAL NO. ______ OF 2023

BETWEEN:

XXXXXXXX ... Curative Petitioners

AND

YYYYYYY ...Respondents

(FOR INDEX PLEASE SEE INSIDE)

<u>Advocates for the Curative Petitioners :</u> ______________________

I NDEX

Sl.No.	Particulars.	Page Nos.
1.	Office report on limitation.	. . . . .
2.	Synopsis, List of dates & events.	. . . . .
3.	Copy of the Impugned Judgment dated ________ passed by this Hon'ble Court in Review Petition No. ________ of 2023.	. . . . .
4.	Certificate of Senior Advocate.	. . . . .
5.	Curative Petition with Affidavit.	. . . . .
6.	**ANNEXURES**	. . . . .
7.	**I.A. No. OF 2023** Application for interim relief	. . . . .
10.	**I.A. NO. OF 2023** Application for oral hearing	. . . . .
11.	**I.A. No. OF 20237** Application for urging additional ground with affidavit.	. . . . .

SYNOPSIS & LIST OF DATES AND EVENTS
IN THE SUPREME COURT OF INDIA
EXTRAORDINARY CIVIL APPELLATE JURISDICTION
CURATIVE PETITION (CIVIL) NO. OF 2023
IN
REVIEW PETITION NO. OF 2023
IN
CIVIL APPEAL NO. OF 2023

BETWEEN:

XXXXXXX ... Curative Petitioners

AND

YYYYYY ...Respondents

JAYPRAKASH BANSILAL SOMANI

CERTIFICATE

1. Certified that I have read the contents of the Review Petition No. _______________ of 2023 and the impugned Order by circulation dated _______________ dismissing the said Review Petition and Judgment and Order dated _______________ in Civil Appeal No. _______________ of 2023.

2. This certificate is being issued primarily for the reason that a basic and fundamental error has crept in the judgment dated _______________ in so far as the provisions of _______________have not been pointed out at any stage of the proceeding to this Hon'ble Court. This Hon'ble Court has naturally not adverted to the said provisions.

3. I certify that apart from what has been stated above strong reasons exist for this Hon'ble Court to exercise its inherent jurisdiction and entertain the Curative Petition seeking reconsideration of its impugned Order dated _______________ passed by circulation in the Review Petition in order to cure a grave miscarriage of justice.

4. The Curative Petition raises, inter alia, a ground that in making its Order and Judgment, dated _______________the impugned judgment does not disturb the judgment of this Hon'ble Court dated _______________ and ignores the specific provisions of _______________Act. Further, this Hon'ble Court has instead gone into the question of _______________. Further, the question of giving documentary evidence by way of Power of Attorney was the law of the State and neither the Petitioners nor the Tribunal could challenge that position. While reversing that law, this Hon'ble Court ought to have remanded the matter to _______________.

5. I certify that these issues would constitute a very strong reason for this Hon'ble Court to entertain this Curative Petition and set aside the grave miscarriage of justice caused by the impugned order of the Court.

6. It is further certified that the ground mentioned in para 2 above was not urged at any stage but since it is a statutory provision conferring right on women therefore it is taken here. Apart from this ground all other grounds taken in the Curative Petition had also been taken in the Review Petition. The Review Petition has been annexed to the Curative Petition as Annexure-A.

7. That I have read the Judgment of this Hon'ble Court in the case of Rupa Ashok Hurra Vs. Ashok Hurra reported in (2002) 4 SCC 388 and certify that the Curative Petition fulfils the requirements of that Judgment.

____

Senior Advocate

New Delhi.

Filed on:

IN THE SUPREME COURT OF INDIA
EXTRAORDINARY CIVIL APPELLATE JURISDICTION
CURATIVE PETITION NO. OF 2023
IN
REVIEW PETITION NO. _______ of 2023
IN
CIVIL APPEAL NO. _____________ OF 2023

BETWEEN :

XXXXXXXXXXXXX Curative Petitioner (original Appellant in Civil Appeal)

A N D

YYYYYYYYY Contesting Respondent

To

Hon'ble the Chief Justice and other

Subordinate Judges of the

Hon'ble Supreme Court of India

The humble Petition of the Petitioners above named :

MOST RESPECTFULLY SHOWETH:

1. The present Curative Petition is directed against the Order dated ___________ passed by this Hon'ble Court by circulation in Review Petition (Civil) No. _______of 2023, seeking review of the impugned Judgment & Order dated ______ passed by this Hon'ble Court in Civil Appeal No. _______ of 2023, whereby, this Hon'ble Court vide a brief Order has dismissed the Review Petition. A copy of the Review Petition (Civil) No. _______of 2023 is annexed hereto and marked as Annexure – 1. Copy of the Judgment and Order dated _____________ passed by this Hon'ble Court in Civil Appeal No ____________of 2023 is annexed hereto and marked as Annexure-2.

2. It is pertinent to mention here that after the order dated _______ was passed in the Review Petition, ...

3. This Curative Petition seeks to invite the kind attention of this Hon'ble Court to the grave injustice, which has been caused in the present case

which makes it a rarest of rare case requiring a reconsideration to set right the miscarriage of justice. The impugned judgment dated _______ has impinged upon the constitutional right of life and liberty of the Petitioner who has been .... Further, the review order does not disturb the judgment of this Hon'ble Court and ignores the specific provisions of ....Act. In its impugned judgment this Hon'ble Court has gone into an inquiry regarding ....

4. The main points for the consideration of this Hon'ble court in the present petition are as follows:

(Mention all relevant and necessary issue as per the case)

5. The facts leading to the filing of the present petition are as under: -

(i) ....

(ii) ....etc.

6. The petitioners beg to submit that inasmuch as the points raised by the petitioner were not considered by this Hon'ble Court, there is an error apparent on the face of the record. The present Curative Petition fulfils the requirements of the Judgment of this Hon'ble Court in Rupa Ashok Hurra Vs. Ashok Hurra reported in (2002) 4 SCC 388.

7. Accordingly the present Curative Petition is being filed raising the following grounds, which are taken without prejudice to one another.

(Mention all reasonable, relevant and necessary grounds as per the case)

8. That the present petition is filed bonafide and in the interest of justice. The Petitioners have not filed any other Curative Petition against the Order dated ___________ passed by this Hon'ble Court by circulation, in Review Petition (Civil) No. _______of 2023, seeking review of the impugned Judgment & Order dated _______ passed by this Hon'ble Court in Civil Appeal No.___________ of 2023; before this Hon'ble Court.

9. This Hon'ble Court may kindly be pleased to grant an opportunity of hearing to the Curative Petitioners as the consequences of the order dated __________ and _______________ on the Curative Petitioners are grave.

<u>PRAYER</u>

In the aforementioned facts, circumstances and submissions, it is most respectfully prayed that this Hon'ble Court may graciously be pleased to:

a) Allow the present Curative Petition;

b) Recall the Order dated _______________ passed by this Hon'ble Court by circulation, in Review Petition (Civil) No. _______ of 2023 and the Judgment & Order dated ___________ passed by this Hon'ble Court in Civil

Appeal No. _________ of 2023;

c) in the event prayer (a) and (b) above are allowed, remit the matter to _______ for fresh enquiry and the Curative petitioners be permitted to depose within shortest possible time.

d) pass such other or further Orders as this Hon'ble Court may deem fit and proper in the circumstances of the case.

AND FOR THIS ACT OF KINDNESS THE PETITIONERS AS IN DUTY-BOUND SHALL EVER PRAY.

Filed by

____

Advocates for the Curative Petitioners

Drawn on: _________

New Delhi

Filed on: _________

IN THE SUPREME COURT OF INDIA

EXTRAORDINARY CIVIL APPELLATE JURISDICTION

I.A. No. ___________ of 2023

IN

CURATIVE PETITION NO. OF 2023

IN

REVIEW PETITION NO. _____ OF 2023

IN

CIVIL APPEAL NO. ______ OF 2023

<u>**BETWEEN**</u>**:**

XXXXXXXX ....Curative Petitioners

AND

YYYYYYYY ....Respondents

<u>**APPLICATION ON BEHALF OF THE**</u>

<u>**CURATIVE PETITIONERS FOR INTERIM RELIEF**</u>

To

Hon'ble the Chief Justice and his

Hon'ble Companion Justices of the

Hon'ble Supreme Court of India.

The humble Application of the

Petitioner abovenamed-

<u>**MOST RESPECTFULLY SHEWETH**</u>

1. The accompanying Curative Petition is directed against the Order dated _____________ passed by this Hon'ble Court by circulation in Review Petition (Civil) No. _____________, seeking review of the impugned Judgment & Order dated __________ passed by this Hon'ble Court in Civil Appeal No. _____________. By the said order dated _______________, the review petition was dismissed. That the contents of the accompanying Curative Petition are not being repeated herein for the sake of brevity and may be read as part of this Application.

1. That the Curative Petition seeks to invite the kind attention of the Hon'ble Court to the facts that raise vital issues and highlight grave miscarriage of justice.

1. It is respectfully submitted that strong reasons exist for this Hon'ble Court to exercise its inherent jurisdiction and entertain the accompanying Curative Petition seeking reconsideration of its impugned Order dated _______________ passed in the Review Petition in order to cure a grave miscarriage of justice.

4. The Curative Petition raises, inter alia, raises a ground that the .... It is respectfully submitted that thus the impugned Orders dated _______________ and _______________ ought to be stayed.

5. The Curative Petitioners have a strong *prima facie* case and is hopeful of ultimately succeeding in the Curative Petition. The balance of convenience is also in the favour of the Curative Petitioners and that grave and irreparable loss and injury would be caused to the Curative Petitioners in case operation of the Impugned Order dated ___________ in Review Petition (C) No. ___________ and _______________ in Civil Appeal No. _____________ is not stayed.

5. In the circumstances, it is most respectfully prayed that the Hon'ble Court may be pleased to grant the following interim relief: -

a) That pending consideration of this Curative Petition the operation of the Impugned Order dated ___________ in Review Petition (C) No. _______________ and ___________ in Civil Appeal No. ___________ be stayed; and

b) that pending the decision in Curative Petition, the Respondent No. 1 be restrained from dealing with or alienating the Residential Property .... or creating any third party rights thereon;

c) pass such other or further Orders as this Hon'ble Court may deem fit and proper in the circumstances of the case.

Filed by:

____

Advocates for the Curative Petitioners

New Delhi:

Dated:

IN THE SUPREME COURT OF INDIA
EXTRAORDINARY CIVIL APPELLATE JURISDICTION
I.A. No. _____________ of 2023 IN
CURATIVE PETITION NO. OF 2023 IN
REVIEW PETITION NO. ________ OF 2023 IN
CIVIL APPEAL NO._______ OF 2023

BETWEEN:

XXXXXXX ....Curative Petitioners

AND

YYYYYYY ....Respondents

APPLICATION SEEKING ORAL HEARING

To

Hon'ble the Chief Justice and his

Hon'ble Companion Justices of the

Hon'ble Supreme Court of India.

The humble Application of the

Petitioners abovenamed-

MOST RESPECTFULLY SHEWETH

1.The accompanying Curative Petition is directed against the Order dated _________ passed by this Hon'ble Court by circulation in Review Petition (Civil) No. ___________ of 2023, seeking review of the impugned Judgment & Order dated ____________ passed by this Hon'ble Court in Civil Appeal No. ____________ of 2023. By the said order dated ____________, the review petition was dismissed. That the contents of the accompanying Curative Petition are not being repeated herein for the sake of brevity and may be read as part of this Application.

2. That the Petitioner has raised a ground in the curative petition that this Hon'ble Court did not advert to the provisions of Section

________________ Act. This section was enacted to confer full and absolute ____ This ground is very pertinent for the purposes of deciding the instant case and hence the Petitioners herein seeks the liberty of this Hon'ble Court to raise the same.

PRAYER

In the circumstances it is most respectfully prayed that this Hon'ble Court may be pleased to –

a) permit the Petitioners to raise the abovementioned ground at the time of hearing the instant Curative Petition; and

b) pass such other and further order or orders as may be deemed just and proper on the facts and in the circumstances of the case.

AND FOR THIS ACT OF KINDNESS, THE PETITIONER, AS IN DUTY BOUND, SHALL EVER PRAY.

Drawn and filed by :

____

Advocates for the Petitioners
New Delhi:
Dated:

TRANSFER PETITION UNDER SECTION 406 OF THE CRIMINAL PROCEDURE CODE READ WITH ORDER XXXIX OF THE SUPREME COURT RULES, 2013.

IN THE SUPREME COURT OF INDIA
CRIMINAL ORIGINAL JURISDICTION
TRANSFER PETITION (CRL.) NO. _____________ of 2023
<u>IN THE MATTER OF:</u>
XXXXXX ... Petitioners
<u>VERSUS</u>
YYYYYY ... Respondent
-: *W I T H* :-

CRL. M. P. NO. OF 2023
Application for exemption from filing official English translation
{ For Index Please See Inside }
Advocate for the Petitioners: _____________

<u>**INDEX**</u>

Sl.No.	Particulars		Page Nos.
1.	Check List	. . . . .	
2.	List of Dates &Events	. . . . .	
3.	Transfer Petition (Criminal) with Affidavit	. . . . .	
4.	**ANNEXURES**		
		. . . . .	
5.	**CRL. M.P.NO. OF 2023.** Application for exemption from filing official English translation.	. . . . .	

<u>**SYNOPSIS & LIST OF DATES AND EVENTS**</u>
IN THE SUPREME COURT OF INDIA
CRIMINAL ORIGINAL JURISDICTION
TRANSFER PETITION (CRL.) NO. _____________ of 2023

<u>**IN THE MATTER OF**</u>:-

XXXXXXXX .. Petitioner

<u>Versus</u>

YYYYYYYY .. Respondents

<u>**Transfer Petition under Section 406 of the Criminal Procedure Code read with Order XXXIX of the Supreme Court Rules, 2013**</u>

TO

THE HON'BLE THE CHIEF JUSTICE OF INDIA AND

HIS COMPANION JUSTICES OF THE

HON'BLE SUPREME COURT OF INDIA

The humble petition of the Petitioners above named:-

<u>**MOST RESPECTFULLY SHOWETH:**</u>

1.This Transfer Petition under Section 406 of the Criminal Procedure Code read with Order XXXIX of the Supreme Court Rules, 2013, seeks the transfer of the following criminal cases pending against the Petitioner in the Special Courts, (CBI), AHD, at Patna and Ranchi to the competent courts outside the States Bihar and Jharkand:-

<u>Cases pending against the Petitioner</u>:-

i. ....
ii. ....
iii. ....
iv. ....
v. .....etc.

2. The transfer is sought in the interests of justice under the following circumstances.

3.The Petitioner is the _________________, and is presently a ________________.

4. The aforementioned cases are pending at different stages of trial in the courts of Patna (Bihar) and Ranchi (Jharkand).

5. That the aforementioned cases have been filed against the Petitioner at the instance of, as well as due to the false propaganda, of the political rivals of the Petitioners.

FACTS OF THE CASE:-

6. ....
....
....
....

7. It is therefore just and necessary and expedient that in the interests of Justice all the aforementioned criminal cases pending against the petitioners in the States of Bihar and Jharkhand are transferred to the competent criminal courts outside Bihar and Jharkhand to ensure fair and impartial trial of the petitioners herein in the aforementioned cases filed against them.

8. The Petitioners state that no other Transfer Petition has been filed by them before this Hon'ble Court.

PRAYER

In the aforementioned facts and circumstances, it is respectfully prayed that this Hon'ble Court may be pleased to:-

a) transfer the under-mentioned criminal cases pending against the Petitioners herein to the Criminal Courts of competent jurisdiction outside the States of Bihar and Jharkhand, in the interests of justice:

A) <u>Cases pending against the Petitioner :-</u>

i. ....

ii. ....

iii. ....

iv. ....

v. ....

b) pass such other and further order(s) as this Hon'ble Court may deem fit and necessary in the facts and circumstances of the case and in the interests of justice.

Settled by Drawn & Filed By:

(_______________) (__________________)

Senior Advocate Advocates for the Petitioners
Place: New Delhi.
Filed on: ____.

TRANSFER APPLICATION UNDER SECTION 25 AND 151 OF THE CODE OF CIVIL PROCEDURE READ WITH ORDER XXXLI OF THE SUPREME COURT RULES 2013 AS ALSO UNDER AR

IN THE SUPREME COURT OF INDIA
CIVIL ORIGINAL JURISDICTION
TRANSFER PETITION (C) NO.____________OF 2023
IN THE MATTER OF:

XXXXXX ....PETITIONER

VERSUS

YYYYYYY ....RESPONDENT

Transfer Application under Section 25 and 151 of the Code of Civil Procedure read with Order XXXLI of the Supreme Court Rules 2013 as also under Article 142 of the Constitution of India for transfer of suit being C.S. No. ______________ and any applications and all other papers and proceedings therein pending on the file of the Hon'ble Madras High Court at Chennai in the State of Tamil Nadu to the Debts Recovery Tribunal, III, Mumbai in the State of Maharashtra to be jointly tried and dispose off with O.A. no. ________________ by Debts Recovery Tribunal, III at Mumbai in the State of Maharashtra.

<u>MOST RESPECTFULLY SHOWETH:-</u>

1. The Petitioner is a banking company engaged in the business of banking and holds a valid license duly issued by the Reserve Bank of India ("RBI") and having its offices mentioned in the cause title above. Necessary certificates and license have been issued by the statutory authorities on the new name. However the shareholding pattern and the managerial control of the Petitioner remain unchanged.

2. The Respondent is engaged in the business of manufacture and export of sugar and is one of the leading industries in the state of Tamil Nadu. The registered office of the Respondent is at "________________________".

3. This Petition/Application has been filed for transfer of Suit being C.S. No________________________ and any applications and all other papers and proceedings therein pending on the file of the Hon'ble Madras High Court at Chennai in the State of Tamil Nadu ("Suit"), to the Debts Recovery Tribunal, III, Mumbai in the State of Maharashtra to be jointly tried and dispose off with O.A. no. ________________ by Debts Recovery Tribunal, III, Mumbai in the State of Maharashtra ("Original Application") on the grounds as set out hereunder.

4. Brief facts which are relevant for the purpose of the present Petition/ Application are set out below:

(a) ....

(b) ....etc.

5. As stated above, the Petitioner has in the past entered into several derivative transactions with Respondents. The said Transaction was a currency option transaction with a Notional Amount of USD 10 million. The said Transaction is of a nature explicitly permitted by RBI and is valid.

GROUNDS *as per the requirement of the case [can mention QOL]*

6. In view of what is stated above and in the interest of justice, equity and good conscience it will be just and proper to order a joint trial by transferring the Suit i.e., C.S. no. ______________(and appeal being OSA ____________)and any petitions/ applications and all other papers and proceedings pending before the Hon'ble Madras High Court at Chennai in the State of Tamil Nadu to the file of the DRT, in the State of Maharashtra

and further directing that the same be treated as a counter claim or set-off or defence in the Original Application i.e., _________________ by the Debts Recovery Tribunal III, Mumbai. Further, it is in the interest of justice, equity and good conscience that pending the hearing and final disposal of this Petition/Application, this Hon'ble Court may be pleased to stay the proceedings being Suit i.e., _______________ (and appeal being OSA ________________)and any petitions/ applications and all other papers and proceedings therein on the file of the Hon'ble Madras High Court at Chennai in the State of Tamil Nadu. It is submitted that if the stay of the Suit and any petitions/ applications and all other papers and proceedings as prayed for is not granted, the Hon'ble Madras High Court at Chennai may proceed with the trial of the Suit and any petitions/ applications and all other papers and proceedings and the entire purpose and objective of making this Petition/Application and the reliefs sought therein would be defeated and/or frustrated.

PRAYERS:

In view of the above facts and circumstances the Petitioner most respectfully prays that:

(a) this Hon'ble Court may be pleased to pass an order for transfer of Suit being C.S. No. ___________ titled as _________________ and any applications and all other papers and proceedings therein pending on the file of the Hon'ble Madras High Court on it ordinary original civil jurisdiction in the State of Tamil Nadu, to the Debts Recovery Tribunal, III, Mumbai in the State of Maharashtra to be jointly tried and disposed off with _______________ titled as_____________________ pending on the file ofDebts Recovery Tribunal, III, Mumbai in the State of Maharashtra and directing that it be treated as a cross suit or counter- claim or a defence against the claim of the Petitioner pending on the file of the Hon'ble Debts Recovery Tribunal, III, Mumbai;

(b) for such other reliefs and prayers as this Hon'ble Court deems fit in the facts and circumstances of the case;

Petition drawn by

FILED BY :

____

Advocates for the Petitioner

Drawn on:

New Delhi:

Dated:

• 79 •

CHAPTER SIXTEEN

COUNTER AFFIDAVIT ON BEHALF OF RESPONDENT

IN THE SUPREME COURT Of INDIA
CIVIL APPELLATE JURISDICTION
SPECIAL LEAVE PETITION (CIVIL) NO. __________ OF 2023
<u>**IN THE MATTER OF:**</u>
XXXXXXX ...Petitioner
Versus
YYYYYYY ...Respondents

<u>COUNTER AFFIDAVIT ON BEHALF OF RESPONDENT NO. <u>1</u></u>

I, ________________ S/o ________________ aged ______years having my office at ______________________ presently at New Delhi do hereby solemnly affirm and state as under:

1. I am the duly constituted Attorney on behalf of Respondent No.1 and Respondent No.2 in the above petition and am conversant with the facts and circumstances of the case and as such am competent to swear this affidavit.

2. I have read over and understood the contents of the List of Dates and Events and the SLP filed by the Petitioner and I am aware of what is stated therein. At the outset, I deny all the averments, submissions, statements and allegations made therein except those that are specifically admitted hereinafter to be true and correct.

3. The subject matter of the present proceedings is the __________________________________.

4. Before dealing with the para-wise comments on the questions of law and the grounds set out by the Petitioner in the instant SLP, the answering

Respondent craves leave of this Hon'ble Court to set out its preliminary objections and submissions as under:

I.PRELIMINARY OBJECTIONS :

5. At the outset, it is submitted that the present SLP is premised on the basis that special equities are created in favour of Respondent No. 4 and Respondent No.5, although, both the Petitioners and Respondents No.4 & 5 herein, were well aware of the orders passed by the Division Bench of the Hon'ble High Court in their presence wherein vide order dated 27th July 2007 the Bombay High Court made it clear that, *"...In the meanwhile the extension/entering into fresh agreement with Respondent No. 4 & 5 by Respondent No.2 shall be subject to the direction that may be passed in the present petition and finalisation of the contract in favour of the said Respondents will be of no consequences"* . Further vide another order dated 27th February 2008, the Hon'ble Division Bench of the Bombay High Court, made it abundantly clear that " ..... *It is made clear that the parties would not be entitled to claim any equities in the matter"*. Pursuant to above orders passed by the High Court the Petitioner and the Respondent Nos. 4 and 5 went ahead with the implementation of the contract and therefore now after the Hon'ble Bombay High Court having come to the conclusion thereby setting aside the works contract awarded by the Petitioners, it is not open to the Petitioners or Respondent No.4 & 5 to claim special equities on the ground of money invested by them or the amount of work done by them. It is further submitted that the work done under the new contract by the Respondent No.4 & 5 was done at their sole risks and cost therefore they should bear the consequences thereof.

6. It is further submitted that order dated 27th July 2007 and order 27th February 2008 have become final and binding as the same have not be challenged by the Petitioners and the Respondent No. 4 and 5. It is therefore not open for the Petitioner or the Respondent No.4 and Respondent No.5 to challenge the same or claim compensation when the actions of the Respondents were at their own risks and costs. The Petitioners and Respondent No.4 and No.5 are as such estopped in law to claim otherwise.

7. The Petitioner cannot approbate and reprobate by taking contradictory stands. It was initially the Petitioners case before the Hon'ble High Court that the present second Contract awarded to Respondent No.4 & 5 is just an extension of the earlier contract as is also stated in the acceptance letter sent to the Respondent Nos. 4 and 5 however at the later stage the Petitioner in its affidavit before the Hon'ble High Court admits

that the present contract awarded to the Respondent No.4 & No.5 though referred to as an extension, is in fact altogether a new contract with new terms. The present SLP deserves to be dismissed on this ground alone.

8. The impugned action of the Petitioner is in contravention of Section 460 (M) of MMC Act 1888 and it has acted arbitrarily beyond the ambit of their permissible jurisdiction and therefore the act of the awarding the contract by Petitioner without inviting tender is ultra virus and is illegal and deserves to be set aside, therefore, it is submitted interference with the impugned judgment is not called for.

II.PRELIMINARY SUBMISSIONS:

9. At the outset, it is submitted that for the sake of convenience the Respondent herein is briefly setting out the contracts and scheme introduced by the Petitioner. Initially, in December 2005 the Petitioner had floated a tender for "advertising rights on existing bus que shelters'. In the said tender the Bombay City was divided into three zones, the City, Western Suburbs and Eastern Suburbs. The term of the contract was to end on 31.12.2008 irrespective of date of commencement of individual lots. The said term was extendable for a further period of one year i.e. ending latest by 31.12.2009. The Respondent herein had also participated in the said tender, which was finally awarded to the Respondent Nos.4 and 5 herein being the highest bidders. It is pertinent to note that respondents were second highest bidders for Western Zone and City Zone, Bennet Coleman & Co(Respondent No 4) by merely Rs 59 lacs approximately for the City Zone & Rs 110 lacs for the Western Suburbs.

10. That subsequently, the Petitioners in December 2006 floated a scheme and called it 'First Finder Scheme'. Under the said scheme, "the existing Bus Poles were to be replaced by modernized Bus Que Shelters and for display of advertisements thereto". Under the FFS the Bus Poles were identified and were given to a Party on the basis of the application for a period of ten years. The difference between this scheme and the earlier contract was that the present scheme the successful candidate had to build new modernised Bus Que Shelters whereas in the earlier contract the successful bidders were given right to advertise on the existing Bus Que Shelters. The present scheme poised constraints like space constraints, time consuming (as altogether new structures had to be built, including foundation etc) and less lucrative locations. It is for this very reason the Respondent No.4 and Respondent No.5 did not even participate in the present scheme. The Respondent herein had applied for 200 poles out of the

200 poles Respondent was initially awarded 22 poles but later 10 more bus poles for development were awarded to the Respondent. In all there were 2,384 bus poles under this scheme, out of which only 483 bus poles were awarded out of 2136 applications received.

III. <u>LEGAL SUBMISSIONS:</u>

11. It is trite of law that all contracts by the Government/ State or by an instrumentality of the State should be granted only by Public Auction or by inviting tenders, so that all eligible persons have an opportunity to bid in the auction process and to ensure that there is total transparency in order to inspire Public confidence. It is cardinal principle of law that the State should not give contracts by private negotiations but by Public auction or by public tendering to get the maximum price and to ensure fairness.

12. In the case of *Kasturi Lal V/s State of Jammu & Kashmir* (1980 (4) SCC 1) this Hon'ble Court has held in paragraphs 10 to 12 & 14 that while awarding contracts the State has to exercise its discretion for the public good and not arbitrarily. The action must satisfy the twin tests of reasonableness and public interest or else the action would be invalid.

13. This Hon'ble Court had further held in *Harminder Singh Arora v/s Union of India* **1986 (3) SCC 247** has held that where a Public Authority or State chooses to invite Tenders, then it must abide by the conditions laid down in the Tender notice and where the terms are changed, the bidders under the original terms ought to be allowed to submit fresh offers in conformity with the new terms.

14. The Supreme Court in the case of *Mahesh Chandra v/s Regional Manager, UP Financial Corporation & Anr.* **(1993) 2 SCC 279** has held that in the case of any transactions involving public property, a public auction is universally recognised to be the best and most fair method. The calling of tenders to execute works, award contracts, etc. can also be resorted to if a public auction is not possible. However, the Hon'ble Supreme Court has gone on to expressly state that "private negotiations" should always be avoided by the public authority as it cannot withstand public gaze. Also, every effort must be made to get the maximum price for the State in a Government contract.

15. The Supreme Court in the case of *Sachidanand Pandey & Anr. v/s State of West Bengal & Ors.* **(1987) 2 SCC 295** has held that the ordinary rule while dealing with state-owned or public-owned property is to do so by public auction or by inviting tenders. Only where there are compelling reasons should there be a departure from this general rule and even then,

the reasons for departure must be rational and not suggestive of discrimination. This Hon'ble Court has expressly held that *"Nothing should be done which gives an impression of bias, jobbery or nepotism".*

16. The Supreme Court in the case of *Life Insurance Corporation of India & Anr. v/s Consumer Education & Research Centre & Ors.* **(1995) 5 SCC 482** held that *"..In the sphere of contractual relations the State, its instrumentality, public authorities or those whose acts bear insignia of public element, action to public duty or obligation are enjoined to act in a manner that is fair, just and equitable after taking objectively all the relevant options into consideration and in a manner that is reasonable, relevant and germane to effectuate the purpose for public good and in general public interest and it must not take any irrelevant or irrational factors into consideration or appear arbitrary in its decision. Duty to act fairly is part of fair procedure envisaged under Articles 14 and 21. Every activity of the public authority or those under public duty or obligation must be informed by reason and guided by the public interest."*

17. Moreover, it is submitted that the new contract awarded to the Respondent No.4 and 5 is in contravention to the mandate of statutory provisions as provided under Section 460 (M) of the MMC Act, 1888, which clearly states that for tenders involving expenditure exceeding Rs.50,000/-, before entering into any contract, the General Manager has to give notice by an advertisement for inviting tenders in local newspapers. In the present case, there was no resolution passed by the BEST Committee under section 460(M) authorising the General Manager to enter into a contract without inviting tenders. The only approval given by the BEST Committee was under Section 460 (K) (e) of the MMC, Act 1888 not under Section 460 (M) of MMC Act, 1888 as envisaged. It is submitted that the approval under section 460 K(e) of the MMC Act 1888, is required when there is a variance in the earlier contract which exceeds Rs. 10 lacs. In the facts of the present case such a approval is not required since the award of the contract is clearly not a variance in the earlier contreact but is infact a new contract in itself with new terms and conditions. The fact that the contract is not an extension but a new contract is also admitted by the Petitioner herein in its Counter Affidavit filed in the Writ Petition before the Hon'ble High Court.

2. REPLY TO THE QUESTIONS OF LAW

At the outset, it is denied that the present SLP raises any substantial question of law to be decided by this Hon'ble Court.

(i) With regard to (i) it is submitted that the High Court did not err in interfering with the action of the Petitioner in awarding the conteract to

Respondent no. 4 and 5 as the same was mala fide, illegal and without any sanction of law.

(ii) & (iii) With regard to (ii) &(iii) it is submitted that the Petitioner herein in granting the contract to the Respondent No. 4 and 5 ignored the statutory provisions of the MMC Act, 1988 and acted beyond the powers conferred to it under the said Act. The High Court was right in law in quashing and setting aside the contract awarded to the Respondent No. 4 & 5. It is submitted that the Section 460 (M) of the MMC Act, 1988 clearly provides that in case a contract involves an expenditure of more than Rs. 50000/- the General Manager, before entering into such contract has to give notice by advertisement in a local newspaper inviting tenders for such contract. Though the provisio to the said section allows the General Manager to enter into a contract for the purpose of the undertaking without inviting tenders if the BEST Committee has passed a Resolution to that effect. In the resent case neither the Petitioner invited any fresh tenders before awarding the same to the Respondent No. 4 & 5 nor have they under any of their Board Resolutions granted permission to the General Manager as contemplated under the provisio to section 460 (M) and as such the action is in violation of section 460(M) of the MMC Act, 1888. The only approval granted by the committee was in terms of section 460 (K)(e) of the Act in the meeting held on 12.6.2007 approving the note dated 8.06.2007. It is submitted that the approval granted under section 460 (K)(e) does not have any applicability with regard to the new contracts granted to Respondent No. 4 & 5 since the section applies to any variation in the existing contract. It is submitted that contract given to Respondent No. 4& 5 was clearly a new contract and cannot be said to be variation in the earlier contact dated 31.3.2005. Moreover, the Petitioner has themselves in their Affidavit admitted that though the award letters refers to the extensions of licenses, in reality it is altogether a new contract awarded in favour of Respondent No. 4 & 5 w.e.f. 1.10.2007.

(iv) With regard to (iv) it is submitted that the action of the Petitioner herein is not only contrary to the statutory and settled law but also against the general public interest at large. It is submitted that the new contract has been illegally awarded to the Respondent No.4 & 5 to sub serve their private commercial interest as opposed to the Public interest which would have been better served had the present Contract was awarded after following due process of law, and would have in fact generated more revenues for the Petitioner.

(v) With regard to (v) it is submitted that the Judicial Review is to be applied in administrative decisions making process of the government to award a contract to a party when the decision making process, as in the present case, is arbitrary, illegal and suffers from procedural impropriety. This Hon'ble Court in Reliance Energy Ltd. & Anr vs. Maharashtra State Road Development Corporation Ltd. & Ors. reported in (2007) 8 SCC 1 has held that in the matter of judicial review the basic test is to see whether there is any infirmity in the decision making process and not in the decision itself. His means that the decision maker must understand correctly the law that regulates his decision making power and he must give effect to it. Otherwise it may result in illegality. The principle of judicial review cannot be denied even in contractual matters of nature in which the Government exercises its contractual powers, but judicial review is intended to prevent arbitrariness and it must be exercised in larger public interest.

(vi) With regard to (vi) it is submitted that all contracts by the Government/ State or by an instrumentality of the State should be granted only by Public Auction or by inviting tenders, so that all eligible persons have an opportunity to bid in the auction process and to ensure that there is total transparency in order to inspire Public confidence. It is cardinal principle of law that the State should not give contracts by private negotiations but by Public auction or by public tendering to get the maximum price and to ensure fairness. The Respondent herein craves leave of this Hon'ble Court to refer to the relevant casc laws at the time of argument.

(vii) &(viii) With reference to (vii) &(viii) it is submitted that the contract awarded by the Petitioner corporation was not in accordance with the provisions of section 460 of the MMC Act, 1888. The Respondent herein reiterates what is stated in paras (ii) & (iii) above.

(ix) It is submitted that the principle of judicial review, the basic test is to see whether there is any infirmity in the decision making process and not just the decision itself, is equally applicable to the government contractual matters as the principle of judicial review is intended to prevent arbitrariness and it must be exercised in larger public interest. This Hon'ble Court in Reliance Enegy Ltd. & Anr vs. Maharashtra State Road Development Corporation Ltd. & Ors. reported in (2007) 8 SCC 1 has reiterated the law on the aspect of judicial review of an administrative action relating to the award of contracts by the government.

(x),(xi) &(xii) With regard to (x),(xi) &(xii), it is submitted that the decision of awarding the contract to he Respondent No. 4 &5 by private negotiations and without inviting tenders was not only irrational but also arbitrary and against the public interest. It was clearly in violation of the provisions of the statutory laws i.e. MMC Act, 1888 as well as against the settled law that all contracts by the Government/ State or by an instrumentality of the State should be granted only by Public Auction or by inviting tenders, so that all eligible persons have an opportunity to bid in the auction process and to ensure transparency in the actions of government and fairness and also so that the Government gets the highest price for its projects.

(xiii) With regard to (xiii) it is submitted that the Petitioner Corporation is governed by the provisions of the MMC Act, 1888 and it cannot in any manner overrule the powers and procedure prescribed therein and act in an arbitrary manner dehorse the provisions contained therein. It is submitted that in the present case the Petitioner corporation has by privately negotiating with the Respondent Nos. 4 & 5 awarded the contract to them. It is submitted that the submission made by the Petitioner that the said contract is in public interest and is more beneficial to the Petitioner is false and the Petitioner has not been able to prove the same on merits. On the contrary it is submitted that had the corporation floated tenders for the contract, which it ought to have, the Petitioner would have earned more revenue. The respondent further submits that based upon the terms of the contract between the Petitioner and Respondent Nos. 4 and 5 the Petitioner stands to lose an amount of Rs.2,033,318,985.60 (approximately Rs.203 Crore) as revenue shortfall due to the various terms of the renewal which are different from the earlier contract and also from the First Finders Scheme including the categorisation of non saleable bus stops, the lack of any escalated payments, non collection of further security guards etc. A chart showing the revenue loss which the Petitioner will accrue as a result of the arbitrary terms of the contract, on the recommendation of the Respondent No. 4and 5, is annexed herewith and marked as **Annexure R -1**.

(xiv) With regard to (xiv) it is submitted that the approval given by the Petitioner to the Respondent Nos. 4 and 5 was not in accordance with the due process of law. The Respondent herein reiterates what is stated in legal submissions above.

(xv) With regard to (xv) it is submitted that the BEST Committee never passed a Resolution under section 460 (M) of the MMC Act. The only approval granted by the committee was in terms of section 460 (K) (e) of the Act in the meeting held on 12.6.2007 approving the note dated 8.06.2007. It is submitted that the approval granted under section 460 (k)(e) does not have any applicability with regard to the new contracts granted to Respondent No. 4 & 5 since the section applies to any variation in the existing contract. The fact, that the said contract was not an extension but a new contract is itself admitted by the Petitioner Corporation in its affidavit.

(xvi) With regard to (xvi) it is submitted that the action of the Petitioner does not have the sanction of section 460(M) of the MMC Act, 1888 as the BEST Committee never passed a Resolution under section 460 (M) of the MMC Act and the High Court has rightly come to the said conclusion.

(xvii) With regard to (xvii) , it is submitted that in the present case the action of the statutory body is arbitrary and illegal either ways i.e. (i) if one goes by the nomenclature mentioned in the document which says that it is an extension of the earlier contract dated 31.3.2005 it is submitted that the extension is illegal as it goes beyond the terms of the original contract. In Haminder Singh Arora vs. UOI reported in (1986) 3 SCC 247 it has been held by this Hon'ble Court that where a Public Authority or State chooses to invite Tenders, then it must abide by the conditions laid down in the Tender notice and where the terms are changed, the bidders under the original terms ought to be allowed to submit fresh offers in conformity with the new terms. (ii) If one goes by the substance of the Administrative action i.e. in substance, it was a new contract, then also the Petitioner corporation ought to have invited fresh tenders from public at large so that all the interested parties get an opportunity to participate in the process and to ensure that the Petitioner gets the highest price for the interest of the public at large. Also, when the Petitioner is entering into a new contract, it has to abide by the provisions and procedure mentioned in section 460(M) of the MMC Act, 1888, which was also not done in the present case.

REPLY TO THE GROUNDS:

-
-
-
-
-
-
-

REPLY TO GROUNDS FOR INTERIM RELIEF:

....

It is submitted that prayer (C) is wholly based on assumptions and presumptions is not tenable in law. The Petitioner without inviting the bids is assuming that it would have got poor response. In fact by committing itself for 15years without tendering the new contract, the Petitioner is poised to loose more than Rs.203 crores revenue. The new contract could have been awarded through tendering on same terms and conditions. The response to First Finder scheme does not give a right to claim interim relief for a completely new contract awarded arbitrarily and illegally.

The Petitioner has not made out a prima facie case. No irreparable loss or injury shall be caused to the Petitioner if the impugn judgment is affirmed.

No balance of convenience lies in Petitioners favour, in fact the balance of convenience is in favour of the Respondent.

It view of the above preliminary objections, preliminary submissions, legal submissions and reply to questions of law and ground made herein the present Special Leave Petition deserves to be dismissed. No facts which were not pleaded before the courts below has been pleaded in the present affidavit.

DEPONENT

VERIFICATION:

I, the deponent above named do hereby declare that the facts stated in the aforesaid paragraphs are true and correct to the best of my knowledge and no part of it is false and nothing material has been concealed there from.

Verified at Delhi on this the _______ day of _______, 2023.

DEPONENT

MISCELLANEOUS APPLICATIONS APPLICATION FOR EXEMPTION FROM FILING CERTIFIED COPY OF THE IMPUGNED ORDER

IN THE SUPREME COURT OF INDIA
CIVIL APPELLATE JURISDICTION
INTERLOCUTORY APPLICATION NO. OF 2023
IN
SPECIAL LEAVE PETITION (CIVIL) NO. OF 2023

IN THE MATTER OF:

XXXXXXX ....Petitioner

Versus

YYYYYYYY ....Respondents

APPLICATION FOR EXEMPTION FROM FILING CERTIFIED COPY OF THE IMPUGNED ORDER DATED ....

TO

THE HON'BLE CHIEF JUSTICE OF INDIA,

AND HIS COMPANION JUDGES OF THE

HON'BLE SUPREME COURT OF INDIA.

THE HUMBLE PETITION OF THE

PETITIONER ABOVE-NAMED.

<u>MOST RESPECTFULLY SHOWETH</u>:

1. That the petitioner has filed instant Special Leave Petition against the final impugned order dated _____________ in Review Application No. ________________ in Revision Petition No.__________________ passed by the Hon'ble National Consumer Dispute Redressal Commission, New Delhi.

2. It is stated that the petitioner is filing here with the true copy of the impugned order dated _____________________ as the certified original copy of the impugned order was misplaced petitioner herein in the train while they were coming to Delhi.

3. That petitioner has applied for the certified copy of the impugned order but the same is yet to be received.

4. That there is some urgency in the matter and it is therefore prayed that the petitioner may be exempted from filing the certified copy of the impugned order, as and when the Hon'ble Court asks for the certified copy of the impugned order during the hearing, the petitioner shall submit the same.

5. This application is made bonafide and in the interest of justice.

PRAYER

It is most respectfully prayed that this Hon'ble Court may graciously be pleased to:-

(a) exempt the petitioner from filing the certified copy of the final impugned order dated ________________ in Review Application No. 89/11 in Revision Petition No.___________________ passed by the Hon'ble National Consumer Dispute Redressal Commission, New Delhi; and

b) pass such further or other order(s) as this Hon'ble Court may deem fit and proper in the facts and circumstances of the case.

Filed by

(________________)

Advocate for the Petitioner

Filed on: _______________

IN THE SUPREME COURT OF INDIA

CIVIL APPELLATE JURISDICTION

INTERLOCUTORY APPLICATION NO. OF 2023

IN

SPECIAL LEAVE PETITION (CIVIL) NO. OF 2023

<u>IN THE MATTER OF</u>:

XXXXXXX ....Petitioner

Versus

YYYYYYY ....Respondents

APPLICATION FOR CONDONATION OF DELAY

To

The Hon'ble Chief Justice of India, and His Companion
Judges of the Hon'ble Supreme Court of India.

The humble petition of the
Petitioner above-named.

MOST RESPECTFULLY SHOWETH:

1. That the petitioner has filed instant Special Leave Petition against the final impugned order dated ___________ in Review Application No. _____________ in Revision Petition No._________________ passed by the Hon'ble National Consumer Dispute Redressal Commission, New Delhi.

2. That the facts stated in the Special Leave Petition be treated as part and parcel of this application and are not being repeated herein for the sake of brevity.

3. That after the passing of impugned order petitioner contacted the counsel to file the present Special Leave Petition. At the time of handing over brief some important documents were not with the record of the petitioner for which he was asked to bring the same. He brought the documents required for filing the present Special Leave Petition. It also took some time.

4. That the documents were in Hindi and the same were got translated into English, which also took time and thus the delay occurred in filing the present Special Leave Petition.

5. That the delay in filing the special leave petition is due to the aforesaid problem and the delay is neither deliberate nor intentional.

6. That the present application is moved bonafide and in the interest of justice for condonation of delay. If the delay is not condoned then the petitioner will suffer irreparable loss and injuries which cannot be compensated in terms of money.

PRAYER

It is, therefore, most respectfully prayed that this Hon'ble Court may be pleased to:

a) condone the delay of days in filing the present Special Leave Petition against the final impugned order dated ________ in Review Application No. __________ in Revision Petition No.____________ passed by the Hon'ble

National Consumer Dispute Redressal Commission, New Delhi; and
b) pass such further or other order(s) as this Hon'ble Court may deem fit and proper in the facts and circumstances of the case.

Filed by

(_______________)

Advocate for the Petitioner

Filed on: _____________

✿✿✿

APPLICATION FOR CONDONATION OF DELAY

IN THE SUPREME COURT OF INDIA
CIVIL APPELLATE JURISDICTION
INTERLOCUTORY APPLICATION NO. OF 2023
IN
SPECIAL LEAVE PETITION (CIVIL) NO. OF 2023

<u>**IN THE MATTER OF**</u>:

XXXXXXX ....Petitioner

Versus

YYYYYYYY ....Respondents

<u>**APPLICATION FOR PERMISSION TO FILE THE SPECIAL LEAVE PETITION**</u>.

To

The Hon'ble Chief Justice of India, and His Companion
Judges of the Hon'ble Supreme Court of India.

The humble petition of the
Petitioner above-named.

<u>**MOST RESPECTFULLY SHOWETH**</u> :

1. That the petitioner has filed instant Special Leave Petition against the final impugned order dated ____________ in Review Application No. ____________ in Revision Petition No.________________ passed by the Hon'ble National Consumer Dispute Redressal Commission, New Delhi.

2. That the facts stated in the Special Leave Petition be treated as part and parcel of this application and are not being repeated herein for the sake of brevity.

3. That after the passing of impugned order petitioner contacted the counsel to file the present Special Leave Petition. At the time of handing

over brief some important documents were not with the record of the petitioner for which he was asked to bring the same. He brought the documents required for filing the present Special Leave Petition. It also took some time.

4. That the documents were in Hindi and the same were got translated into English, which also took time and thus the delay occurred in filing the present Special Leave Petition.

5. That the delay in filing the special leave petition is due to the aforesaid problem and the delay is neither deliberate nor intentional.

6. That the present application is moved bonafide and in the interest of justice for condonation of delay. If the delay is not condoned then the petitioner will suffer irreparable loss and injuries which cannot be compensated in terms of money.

PRAYER

It is, therefore, most respectfully prayed that this Hon'ble Court may be pleased to:

a) condone the delay of days in filing the present Special Leave Petition against the final impugned order dated _________ in Review Application No. ____________ in Revision Petition No.____________ passed by the Hon'ble National Consumer Dispute Redressal Commission, New Delhi; and

b) pass such further or other order(s) as this Hon'ble Court may deem fit and proper in the facts and circumstances of the case.

Filed by

(____________________)

Advocate for the Petitioner

Filed on: ____________

❧❧❧

CHAPTER NINETEEN

APPLICATION FOR PERMISSION TO FILE THE SPECIAL LEAVE PETITION

IN THE SUPREME COURT OF INDIA
CIVIL APPELLATE JURISDICTION
INTERLOCUTORY APPLICATION NO. OF 2023
IN
SPECIAL LEAVE PETITION (CIVIL) NO. OF 2023

IN THE MATTER OF:

XXXXXXX ....Petitioner

Versus

YYYYYYYY ....Respondents

APPLICATION FOR PERMISSION TO FILE THE SPECIAL LEAVE PETITION.

TO,

HON'BLE CHIEF JUSTICE OF INDIA AND HIS
LORDSHIP'S COMPANION JUSTICES OF THE
SUPREME COURT OF INDIA, NEW DELHI.

THE HUMBLE PETITIONER OF THE
PETITION ABOVE NAMED.

MOST RESPECTFULLY SHOWETH:

That the petitioner is filing present Special Leave Petition under Article 136 of the Constitution of India 1 against the final Judgment and Order dated _______________ passed by the Hon'ble High Court of Judicature at Allahabad, (Lucknow Bench), Lucknow in Writ Petition No. _______________.

That the facts of the case are not repeated hereinafter for the sake of brevity and the same may be read as part and parcel of this application also.

That the petitioner is aggrieved and affected by the impugned judgment and order dated _______________ passed by High Court in Writ Petition No. _________________ because the High Court has seaside the amendment made in L.R. Manual under which the petitioner was engaged by the Government as Assistant District Government Counsel.

That the engagement of petitioner as assistant District Government Counsel has been set aside by the High Court by impugned order and the petitioner was not made party before High Court.

PRAYER:

It is therefore, most respectfully prayed that this Hon'ble Court may be pleased to :

Allow the application for permission to file the Special Leave Petition against the Impugned Judgment and order dated _________________ passed by the Hon'ble High Court of Allahabad Lucknow Benceh, Lucknow in Writ Petition No. _______________.

b. Pass any other or further Order(s) which may be deemed to be just, fit and proper in the facts and circumstances of the case in favour of the petitioner and against the respondents.

Filed By:

(_____________)

Dated. _______________ Advocate for the Petitioners

APPLICATION FOR EXEMPTION FROM FILING OFFICIAL TRANSLATION

IN THE SUPREME COURT OF INDIA
CIVIL APPELLATE JURISDICTION
INTERLOCUTORY APPLICATION NO. OF 2023
IN
SPECIAL LEAVE PETITION (CIVIL) NO. OF 2023

<u>**IN THE MATTER OF**</u>:

XXXXXXX ....Petitioner

Versus

YYYYYYYY ....Respondents

<u>**APPLICATION FOR EXEMPTION FROM FILING OFFICIAL TRANSLATION**</u>

To

The Hon'ble Chief Justice of India, and His Companion

Judges of the Hon'ble Supreme Court of India.

The humble petition of the
Petitioner above-named.

<u>**MOST RESPECTFULLY SHOWETH**</u>:

1. That the petitioner has filed instant Special Leave Petition against the final impugned order dated _________ in Review Application No. __________ in Revision Petition No.__________ passed by the Hon'ble National Consumer Dispute Redressal Commission, New Delhi.

2. That some part of impugned order and Annexure P-2 of the Petition were in Hindi in original. Due to the urgency involved in the matter, the

petitioner had entrusted the work of translation of the some part of impugned order and Annexure P-2 to an advocate practicing in this Hon'ble Court and who is competent and well-versed in both the languages.

3. That it is submitted that it is in the interests of justice that the Petitioners be exempted from filing the official translation of some part of impugned order and Annexure P-2 to the accompanying Special Leave Petition.

<u>PRAYER</u>

In the premises, it is most humbly and respectfully prayed that this Hon'ble Court may graciously be pleased to:

a) exempt the petitioner from filing official translation of some part of impugned order and Annexures P-2 filed with the Special Leave Petition; and

b) pass such further or other order(s) as this Hon'ble Court may deem fit and proper in the facts and circumstances of the case.

Filed by

(_________________)

Advocate for the Petitioner

Filed on: _________________

APPLICATION FOR PERMISSION TO FILE ADDITIONAL DOCUMENT

IN THE SUPREME COURT OF INDIA
CIVIL APPELLATE JURISDICTION
INTERLOCUTORY APPLICATION NO. OF 2023
IN
SPECIAL LEAVE PETITION (CIVIL) NO. OF 2023

IN THE MATTER OF:

XXXXXXX ....Petitioner

Versus

YYYYYYYY ....Respondents

APPLICATION FOR PERMISSION TO FILE ADDITIONAL DOCUMENT:-

TO,

Hon'ble The Chief Justice of India And his
Lordship's other Hon'ble Companion Judges
of the Supreme Court of India

The humble petition of the
petitioners above named

MOST RESPECTFULLY SHOWETH:

1. That the Petitioners above named has filed the aforesaid Special Leave Petition under Article 136 of the Constitution of India against final Judgment and Order dated _____________ in Writ Petition No. _____________ passed by the High Court of Judicature at Allahabad,

Lucknow Bench, Lucknow. The respondent herein has filed counter affidavit of the above said Special Leave Petition . Therefore same are not being the repeated for the sake of brevity.

2. That the respondent herein seek leave of this Hon'ble Court to file the certain Additional documents which have important bearing upon the decision of the case, have been received to the respondent from Chitrakoote Police under the Right to Information Act thus, the same are necessary to be brought on record of the special leave petition.

3. That the very basis of the action taken against the respondent, is the case diary bearing Volume No.______________, dated ____________, in which _____________, then S.H.O. __________________h, while doing investigation of Case Crime No.______________, has mentioned that had the respondent paid due attention to precautions mentioned by him in the said case diary, the unfortunate incident would not have occurred. The typed translated copy of the said case diary has been annexed by the petitioner at page 168 as Annexure No.P-3 of special leave petition and the aforesaid observation of ________________ is available on page 171.

4. That the case of respondent before the Hon'ble High Court is that the then officials of the State Government acted in severe mala fide and arbitrary manner to place the respondent under suspension for the reason that the respondent had been one of the investigating officers in the disproportionate assets case of __________________, .

5. That the report dated __________ (Annexure No.P-5 Para-2, Page No.__________ of SLP) submitted by ___________________, refers the aforesaid observations of _____________ of the Case Diary Volume No._______________ and the same has further been relied upon by all other officials of the department in taking action against the respondent.

6. That it is submitted that the aforesaid documents could not be filed alongwith the Counter Affidavit filed by respondent. However, it is submitted that the documents being filed alongwith this application have for a bearing on the matter in issue. Therefore, it would be would be expedient in the interest of justice to kindly permit the Respondent to place on record the additional documents filed along with this I.A.

PRAYER

It is, therefore, most respectfully prayed that this Hon'ble Court may graciously be pleased to

I. Permit the respondent of file additional documents annexed herewith as Annexure AR-1.
II. Pass such other order or orders as may be deemed fit and proper in the circumstances of the case.

DRAWN AND FILED BY

Drawn on: ________________ (__________________)

Filed on: _____________ Advocate for Respondent.

CHAPTER TWENTY-TWO

AN APPLICATIONFOR CONDONATION OF DELAY IN REFILING THE SPECIAL LEAVE PETITION

IN THE SUPREME COURT OF INDIA
CIVIL APPELLATE JURISDICTION
INTERLOCUTORY APPLICATION NO. OF 2023
IN
SPECIAL LEAVE PETITION (CIVIL) NO. OF 2023

<u>IN THE MATTER OF</u>:

XXXXXXX ....Petitioner

Versus

YYYYYYY ....Respondents

**<u>AN APPLICATION FOR CONDONATION OF DELAY
IN REFILING THE SPECIAL LEAVE PETITION</u>**

To,

THE HON'BLE CHIEF JUSTICE OF INDIA AND

HIS COMPANIOU JUSTICE OF THE

HON'BLE SUPREME COURT OF INDIA

THE HUMBLE APPLICATION OF

THE PETITIONERS ABOVENAMED:

<u>MOST RESPECTFULLY SHEWETH</u>:

That the petitioners have filed the abovementioned Special Leave Petition against the final judgment and order dated ___________ passed by the Hon'ble National Consumer Disputes Redrassel Commission in revision petition no _______________.

1. That the petitioner has stated the facts of the case and the ground arising there from in the accompanying petition and the same may be treated as part and parcel of this Application.

2. That the instant matter has been filed on _____________ and after scrutiny the same was returned to the undersigned for curing defects. The file of the instant case was mixed up with some disposed of files lying in the office of the undersigned and the same placed after a frantic search consequently leading to a short delay.

3. That the delay has occurred in refilling the Special Leave Petition and this delay was unintentional and due to circumstances beyond the control of the petitioner.

<u>**PRAYER**</u>

It is, most respectfully prayed that this Hon'ble Court may be pleased to:

(a) Condoned the delay of days in re-filing the Special Leave Petition from impugned judgment and Final order dated ___________ passed by the Hon'ble National Consumer Disputes Redrassel Commission in revision petition no _________; AND;

(b) Pass such any other or further order as this Hon'ble Court may deem fit and proper in the facts and circumstances of the case.

(_______________)

FILED ON:- ADVOCATE FOR THE PETITIONER

CHAPTER TWENTY-THREE

APPLICATION FOR BAIL

IN THE SUPREME COURT OF INDIA
CRIMINAL APPELLATE JURISDICTION
CRIMINAL MISC. PETITION NO.OF 2023
IN
SPECIAL LEAVE PETITION (CRL.) NO.OF 2023

<u>**IN THE MATTER OF:**</u>

XXXXXXX ..Petitioner

Versus

YYYYYYY ..Respondent

<u>**APPLICATION FOR BAIL**</u>

To

The Hon'ble Chief Justice of India,

and His Companion Judges of the

Hon'ble Supreme Court of India.

The humble petition of the

Petitioners above-named.

<u>**MOST RESPECTFULLY SHOWETH:**</u>

1. That the Petitioner has filed the accompanying Special Leave Petition against the final impugned order dated ________________ passed by the Hon'ble High Court of Madhya Pradesh, Bench at Indore in Criminal Appeal No. ____________.

2. That the facts stated in the Special Leave Petition be treated as part and parcel of this application and are not being repeated herein for the sake of brevity.

That the petitioner has been sentenced to undergo and imprisonment for R.I. for ___________years U/s.__________ of the IPC.

That the petitioner is an old person aged about 70 years and suffering from Cancer.

5. That the petitioner is the only bread earner of his family and his entire family is facing hardship because of the petitioner being inside the jail since the time of his arrest.

6. That the petitioner undertakes to abide the terms and conditions imposed by this Hon'ble Court.

7. That the petitioner on the basis of the accompanying Special Leave petition has full hope and belief to succeed herein before this Hon'ble Court and if the bail is not granted the petitioner will suffer irreparable loss and injury.

8. The present application is being moved bonafide and in the interest of justice.

9. That it is just expedient and necessary in the ends of justice that this Hon'ble Court be graciously pleased to allow this application.

<u>PRAYER</u>

In the premises, it is most humbly and respectfully prayed that this Hon'ble Court may graciously be pleased to:

a) grant bail to the petitioner to the satisfaction of Ld. 8th Addl. Sessions Judge, Indore in S.T. No.____________; and

b) pass such further or other order(s) as this Hon'ble Court may deem fit and proper in the facts and circumstances of the case.

Filed by

____

Advocate for the Petitioner

Filed on: _______________

CHAPTER TWENTY-FOUR

APPLICATION FOR EXEMPTION FROM SURRENDERING

IN THE SUPREME COURT OF INDIA
CRIMINAL APPELLATE JURISDICTION
CRIMINAL MISC. PETITION NO.OF 2023
IN
SPECIAL LEAVE PETITION (CRL.) NO.OF 2023

<u>IN THE MATTER OF:</u>

XXXXXXX ..Petitioner

Versus

YYYYYYY ..Respondent

<u>APPLICATION FOR EXEMPTION FROM SURRENDERING</u>

To

The Hon'ble Chief Justice of India,

and His Companion Judges of the

Hon'ble Supreme Court of India.

The humble petition of the

Petitioners above-named.

<u>MOST RESPECTFULLY SHOWETH:</u>

1. That the Petitioner has filed the accompanying Special Leave Petition against the final impugned order dated ______________ passed by the Hon'ble High Court of Madhya Pradesh, Bench at Indore in Criminal Appeal No. ______________.

2. That the facts stated in the Special Leave Petition be treated as part and parcel of this application and are not being repeated herein for the sake

of brevity.

3. That the petitioner is an innocent and law abiding citizen and also there is no criminal history against him.

4. That the petitioner due to some unavoidable family circumstances has not surrendered in jail as yet as such he is seeking an exemption from surrendering in jail at present.

5. That the petitioner on the basis of the accompanying Special Leave petition has full hope and belief to succeed herein before this Hon'ble Court and if the exemption from surrendering in jail is not allowed the petitioner will suffer irreparable loss and injury.

6. The present application is being moved bonafide and in the interest of justice.

7. That it is just expedient and necessary in the ends of justice that this Hon'ble Court be graciously pleased to allow this application.

<u>PRAYER</u>

In the premises, it is most humbly and respectfully prayed that this Hon'ble Court may graciously be pleased to:

a) exempt the petitioner from surrendering in the present Special Leave Petition ;AND;

b) pass such further or other order(s) as this Hon'ble Court may deem fit and proper in the facts and circumstances of the case.

Filed by

(_________________)
Advocate for the Petitioner

Filed on:_______________

CHAPTER TWENTY-FIVE

PUBLIC INTEREST LITIGATION FORM NO.33 ORDER XXXVIII RULES 12 AND 13 OF SCR, 2013

IN THE SUPREME COURT OF INDIA
EXTRA-ORDINARY ORIGINAL JURISDICTION
WRIT PETITION NO._______________/2023
PUBLIC INTEREST LITIGATION

IN THE MATTER OF:

XXXXXX .....PETITIONER

VERSUS

YYYYY ......RESPONDENT

To,

Hon'ble the Chief Justice of India

and His Companion Judges of the

Supreme Court of India

The Writ Petition of the Petitioner most respectfully showeth:

The petitioner above-named respectfully submits this Petition seeking-

1.Particular of the cause/order against which the petition is made:

(1) Date of Order/ Notification/ Circular/ Policy/ Decision etc.................

(2) Subject-matter brief ....

2.The antecedents of the Petitioner:

(1) That the petitioner ....(give petitioner's social public standing/ professional status and public spirited antecedents; if the

petitioner is a social group or organization,

(2) That present petition under Article 32 of the Constitution of India is being filed by way of public interest litigation and the petitioner has no personal interest (if he has any personal interest, disclose the nature and extent of such interest). The petition is being filed in the interest of...............

(3) That the petitioner is filing the present petition on his own and not at the instance of someone else. The litigation cost, including the advocate's fee and the travelling expense of lawyers, if any, are being borne by the petitioner himself (if not, the petitioner must disclose the source of funds).

3.Facts constituting the cause of action:

Brief facts of the case.

4.Source of information:

Declare the source of information if the statement is based on information or the facts pleaded in the Public Interest Litigation; also whether the applicant has verified the facts personally, if yes, in what manner?

5.Details of remedies exhausted :

The petitioner declares that he has availed all statutory and other remedies.

6.Nature and extent of injury caused or likely to be caused to the public:

Specify concisely about the nature of injury caused or likely to be caused.

7.Nature and extent of personal interest, if any, of the petitioners.

Specify briefly the nature and extent of personal interest, if any

8.Details regarding any civil, criminal or revenue litigation, involving the petitioner or any of the petitioners, which has or could have a legal nexus with the issue (s) involved in the Public Interest Litigation.

Specify the details, if any.

9.Whether issue was raised earlier; if so, what result:

Make a statement/ declaration that the issue raised was neither dealt with nor decided by a Court of law at the instance of the petitioner or to the best of his knowledge, at the instance of any other person and in case such an issue was raised or dealt with, the status or result thereof.

(Also disclose whether in a PIL, any cost has been awarded to or imposed upon the petitioner; and whether any appreciation or stricture has been passed).

10.Whether concerned Government Authority was moved for relief(s) sought in the Petition and if so, with what result:

State whether the petitioner has made any representation in this regard to the concerned authority, if yes, details of such representation and reply, if any, from the authority concerned, along with copies thereof. If not, reason for not making such representation.

11.Grounds :

Specify the grounds precisely and clearly.

12.Grounds for interim relief:

Specify the grounds for interim relief.

13.Main Prayer:

Specify below the relief(s) prayed for.

14.Interim relief, if any:

Give the nature of interim order prayed for, with reason.

Place: ....

Date:...............

Signature

Advocate on record for petitioner

CAVEAT (FORM NO.34)

IN THE SUPREME COURT OF INDIA
CAVEAT APPLICATION NO.______________/2023
IN THE MATTER OF:
XXXXXX .....CAVEATOR
VERSUS
YYYYY ......CAVEATEE
To,
Hon'ble the Chief Justice of India
and His Companion Judges of the
Supreme Court of India

<u>**CAVEAT**</u>

<u>**MOST RESPECTFULLY SHOWETH:**</u>

The caveator above-namcd respectfully begs to submit as under:-

1. That it is expected that the caveatee may prefer any appeal/ petition to the Supreme Court praying for interim relief therein.

2. That the caveator was party to the proceedings before the High Court as ....

3. That the caveator has dispatched a notice of caveat by registered post with acknowledgment due/by courier service, on the person by whom the appeal/ petition has been, or is expected to be filed, furnishing particulars regarding the judgment/order etc. as detailed hereinabove, in respect whereof the caveat is filed.

A receipt evidencing dispatch of the caveat is annexed as annexure.............

4. The postal address of the caveator or his authorized agent.....................

5. It is, therefore, prayed that, in the event of the caveatee preferring such an appeal/ petition within a period of 90 days, with an application seeking any interim relief:-

(a) Notice of lodging of the petition may kindly be given to the caveator.

Signature
Advocate on record for caveator

Place:
Date:

Adv. Jayprakash Somani's Videos On Law

Adv. Jayprakash Somani's Videos on Law on Youtube- 'jaysomani64' channel.

1) SLP in Supreme Court / Special Leave Petitions in the Supreme Court of India

2) Transfer of Civil & Criminal Cases by the Supreme Court of India / Transfer of Matrimonial Cases

3) Appellate Jurisdiction of the Supreme Court of India

4) Jurisdictions of the Supreme Court of India

5) Public Interest Litigation in the Supreme Court of India / PIL in Supreme Court

6) Article 32 Writ Petitions in the Supreme Court of India

7) Bail Matters Top 10 Supreme Court Cases

8) FIR Quashing in High Court & Supreme Court

9) Bail & Anticipatory Bail Matters in Supreme Court

10) Insolvency & Bankruptcy Matters in the Supreme Court

11) Insolvency & Bankruptcy Code 2016 Part 1

12) Insolvency & Bankruptcy Code 2016 Part 2

13) Insolvency & Bankruptcy Code 2016 Part 3

14) Corporate Liquidation Process

15) Supreme Court Rules & Procedures Webinar of 2.5 hour on Zoom

16) RDDBFI Act, 1993 (Introduction)

17) The Indian Contact Act 1872

18) Negotiable Instruments Act (Introduction)

19) How to avoid matrimonial disputes& some more videos

20) SEBI Matters in the Supreme Court

21) Matrimonial Matters: Supreme Court's 20 Case Laws

22) Consumer Matters Supreme Court's 20 Case Laws

23) Service Matters Supreme Court's 20 Case Laws

24) How to Search Lawyer for Your Matter

25) Property Matters Supreme Court's 20 Case Laws

26) Bail Matters: Supreme Court's 20 Case Laws

27) Supreme Court / High Court Vacation Benches

28) 69000 Teacher's Recruitment Matters of UP Government in the Supreme Court

29) Contempt of Court Matters in the Supreme Court

30) Advocate Act's Matters in the Supreme Court

31) Business Law Matters in the Supreme Court

32) Banking Matters in the Supreme Court

33) Labour Law Matters in the Supreme Court

34) Arbitration Matters in the Supreme Court

35) Careers in Law -Zoom Webinar by Adv. Jayprakash Somani

36) Civil Matters in the Supreme Court

37) Consumer Protection Act | Consumer Matters in the Supreme Court

38) Corporate Matters in the Supreme Court

39) Criminal Matters in the Supreme Court

40) Role of Respondent in the Supreme Court of India

41) Motor Vehicle Accident Matters in Supreme Court with case laws

42) Article 131 Original Suits in Supreme Court

43) PIL in Supreme Court/ Public Interest Litigations in the Supreme Court of India'

44) CAB Citizenship Amendment Bill is not Unconstitutional

45) Supreme Court of India Cases & Process – Marathi

46) Legal Services Export / Export of Legal Services

47) Transfer of Matrimonial Cases by the Supreme Court of India

48) Public Interest Litigation PIL

49) The Specific Relief Act (Introduction)

50) Corporate Insolvency Resolution Process CIRP

51) ABMM's Career 5 - Careers in Law

52) Transfer of cases by Supreme Court

53) Writ Petitions in High Court & Supreme Court of India

54) Supreme Court Jurisdictions - Appeals, SLP, Writ Petitions, Transfer, Original, Review, Curative

55) LEGAL INDIA TV Show: Cases Handled in Supreme Court

56) Corporate Liquidation Process

57) Legal Services Export / Export of Legal Services

58) Corporate Laws

59) Election Matters- Supreme Court's 20 Case Laws

60) Companies Act, 2013

62) Competition Act, 2002

63) Banking Matters - Supreme Court's 20 Case Laws

64) Election Matters in the Supreme Court

65) Armed Forces Tribunal Matters in the Supreme Court

66) Compassionate Appointment Service matter

67) Foreign Exchange Management Act FEMA

68) Foreign Trade Policy 2021-26 Proposed

69) Customs Act 1962

70) Narcotic Drugs and Psychotropic Substances Act, 1985 NDPS Act

71) Foreign Trade Development & Regulation Act, 1992

72) How to Search Good Advocate in the Supreme Court of India

73) Sr. Adv Vikas Singh's Interview in Nani Palkhivala Wednesday Law Club

74) Indian Penal Code (I. P. C.)

75) Criminal Procedure Code (Cr. P. C.)

76) Commercial Courts & International Arbitration - by Mr. Jaideep Gupta, Senior Advocate in Nani Palkhivala Wednesday Law Club

77) Sr. Adv Ranji Thomos in Nani Palkhivala Wednesday Law Club

78) Urgent Matters in Supreme Court during vacations

79) 498A Bail Matters in Supreme Court

81) 376 Bail Matters in Supreme Court

82) 302, 304, 307, 308 Bail Matters in Supreme Court

83) 138, 420 Bail Matters in Supreme Court

84) POCSO Act Bail Matters in Supreme Court

85) NDPS Act Bail Matters in Supreme Court

86) What is ED (Enforcement Directorate)?

87) Prevention of Money Laundering Act, 2002 (PMLA Act)

88) Insolvency & Bankruptcy Code- Supreme Court Case Laws. Webinar in Nani Palkhivala Wednesday Law Club

89) What is NCLT & NCLAT?

90) Acquittal from 376- Supreme Court's some case laws in Nani Palkhivala Wednesday Law Club dt 28.7.22

91) Insolvency & Bankruptcy in India

92) Can we file case directly in the Supreme Court?

93) Adv. Anuja Pethia has cleared AOR Exam 2021 with 77% marks - Her interview in Nani Palkhivala Wednesday Law Club

94) Customs Act - Supreme Court Case Laws & Interview of AOR Adv. Anuja Pethia in Nani Palkhivala Law Club.

95) The Uttar Pradesh Public Service Tribunals Act, 1976

96) POCSO Act - Supreme Court Case Laws & Interview of AOR Adv. Shoumendu Mukharji & Adv. Nishant Verma in Nani Palkhivala Law Club.

97) Who Can Trigger CIRP Process Under Insolvency Law of India

98) The Uttar Pradesh Government Servant Discipline and Appeal Rules, 1999

99) CIRP Application Under Sec 7 by FC

100) Information Technology Act 2000

101) Uttar Pradesh Recruitment of Dependants of Government Servants Dying in Harness Rules, 1974

102) Foreign Exchange Management Act 1999 & Supreme Court's Case Laws on FEMA & Leading Case of AOR Exam in Nani Palkhivala Law Club.

103) Arbitration and Conciliation Act 1996 & It's Supreme Court Case Laws in Nani Palkhivala Wednesday Law Club.

104) Narcotic Drugs & Psychotropic Substances Act 1985 (NDPS Act) & It's Supreme Court Case Laws in Nani Palkhivala Wednesday Law Club.

105) Recovery of Debts and Bankruptcy Act 1993

106) Uttar Pradesh Land Revenue Code 2006

107) CIRP Application Under Sec 9 by OC

108) CIRP Application Under Sec 10 by CD

109) Hindu Succession Act, 1956

110) Maharashtra Civil Services Rules, 1981

111) Indian Contract Act, 1872 & Supreme Court's Case Laws" in Nani Palkhiwala Wednesday Law Club

112) Securities and Exchange Board of India Act, 1992 i. e. SEBI Act 1992 & Case Laws on Insiders Trading" in Nani Palkhiwala Wednesday Law Club

113) Moratorium Under Section 14 of IBC, 2016

114) Hindu Marriage Act, 1955

115) Maharashtra Land Revenue Code, 1966

116) 64 Leading Cases of AOR Exam Session 1 :- Cases 1 to16 in Nani Palkhiwala Wednesday Law Club

117) 64 Leading Cases of AOR Exam Session 2: Cases 17 to 32 in Nani Palkhiwala Wednesday Law Club

118) 64 Leading Cases of AOR Examination Session 3: Cases 33 to 48 in Nani Palkhiwala Wednesday Law Club

119) 64 Leading Cases of AOR Exam Session 4: Cases 49 to 64 in Nani Palkhiwala Wednesday Law Club

120) Labour Laws of India: Part 1 - 4 New Labour Law Codes of India

121) New Labour Laws Part 2 The Code on Wages, 2019

122) New Labour Laws Part 3:- The Code on Social Security, 2020

123) Argue in English Fluently & Confidently - Two months online course.

124) SLP Admission in the Supreme Court. 2023 (Hindi)

125) Transfer of Petitions from the Supreme Court (Hindi)

126) Review Petition in the Supreme Court.(Hindi)

127) Recovery of debts from the Company (Hindi)

128) How to search 'Good Insolvency & Bankruptcy Consultant?' (HINDI)

129) Curative Petition in the Supreme Court

130) AFT Appeals in the Supreme Court (HINDI)

131) NCLAT's Appeals in the Supreme Court.

132) Transfer Petition: Which matters can we transfer?

133) SLP Types of SLP in the Supreme court of India (English).

134) Argue in English Fluently and Confidently in the High Court & Supreme Court'.

List Of Adv. Jayprakash Somani's Published Books

1. Supreme Court of India's Leading Case Laws on 'Insolvency & Bankruptcy Code 2016'

2. Bail Matters – Supreme Court's Latest Leading Case Laws

3. Arbitration Matters- Supreme Court's Latest Leading Case Laws

4. Property Matters - Supreme Court's Latest Leading Case Laws

5. Matrimonial Matters- Supreme Court's Latest Leading Case Laws

6. Election Matters- Supreme Court's Latest Leading Case Laws

7. SEBI Matters- Supreme Court's Latest Leading Case Laws

8. Banking Matters- Supreme Court's Latest Leading Case Laws

9. Service Matters- Supreme Court's Latest Leading Case Laws

10. Contempt of Court Matters- Supreme Court's Latest Leading Case Laws

11. Consumer Protection Matters- Supreme Court's Latest Leading Case Laws

12. Corporate Law- Supreme Court's Latest Leading Case Laws

13. Supreme Court's AOR Exam- Leading Cases

14. Armed Force Tribunal - Supreme Court's Latest Leading Case Laws

15. Acquittal From 376 - Supreme Court's Latest Leading Case Laws

16. Negotiable instrument – Supreme Court's Latest Leading Case Laws

17. Contract Act- Supreme Court's Latest Leading Case Laws

18. Insider trading- Supreme Court's Latest Leading Case Laws

19. Foreign Exchange and Management Act- Supreme Court's Latest Leading Case Laws

20. Income Tax Act- Supreme Court's Latest Leading Case Laws

21. Company Law- Supreme Court's Latest Leading Case Laws

22. Competition & Monopoly Matters- Supreme Court's Latest Leading Case Laws

23. Compassionate Appointment- Service Matters- Supreme Court's Latest Leading Case Laws

24. Compulsory Retirement- Service Matters- Supreme Court's Latest Leading Case Laws

25. Voluntary Retirement- Service Matters- Supreme Court's Latest Leading Case Laws

26. Removal/Dismissal/Termination from Service- Supreme Court's Latest Leading Case Laws

27. Seniority- Service Matter- Supreme Court's Latest Leading Case Laws

28. Promotion- Service Matter- Supreme Court's Latest Leading Case Laws

29. Equal Pay for Equal Work- Service Matter- Supreme Court's Latest Leading Case Laws

30. Condition of Service- Service Matter- Supreme Court's Latest Leading Case Laws

31. Customs Act- Supreme Court's Leading Case Laws

32. Information Technology Act- Supreme Court's Leading Case Laws

33. SEC. 125 CR. P. C.- Supreme Court's Leading Case Laws

34. SEC. 498A OF I. P. C.- Supreme Court's Leading Case Laws

35. MOTOR VEHICLE ACT- Supreme Court's Leading Case Laws

36. CONDITION OF SERVICE- SERVICE MATTER- Supreme Court's Leading Case Laws

37. SUSPENSION- SERVICE MATTER- Supreme Court's Leading Case Laws

38. Reservation in SC, ST, OBC- Service Matter- Supreme Court's Leading Case Laws

39. NARCOTIC DRUGS AND PSYCHOTROPIC SUBSTANCES (NDPS) ACT - Supreme Court of India's Latest Leading Case Laws

40. SEC 302 IPC - Supreme Court of India's Latest Leading Case Laws

41. PROTECTION OF CHILDREN FROM SEXUAL OFFENCES ACT (POCSO) - Supreme Court of India's Latest Leading Case Laws

42. PMLA ACT BAIL MATTERS - Supreme Court of India's Leading Case Laws

43. SEC 376 BAIL MATTERS - Supreme Court of India's Leading Case Laws

44. SEC 302 BAIL MATTERS - Supreme Court of India's Leading Case Laws

45. POCSO ACT BAIL MATTERS - Supreme Court of India's Leading Case Laws

46. JUVENILE JUSTICE ACT- Supreme Court of India's Leading Case Laws

47. TRANSFER OF PROPERTY ACT- Supreme Court of India's Leading Case Laws

48. PROFESSIONAL ETHICS OF ADVOCATES- AOR EXAM- SUPREME COURT'S LEADING CASE LAWS

49. WHITE COLLAR CRIME- SUPREME COURT'S LEADING CASE LAWS

50. SEC 302 BAIL MATTERS- SUPREME COURT'S LEADING CASE LAWS

51. SEC 7 IBC 2016 - SUPREME COURT'S LATEST LEADING CASE LAW

52. ADVERSE POSSESSION IN PROPERTY MATTER - SUPREME COURT'S LATEST LEADING CASE LAWS

53. FOOD SAFETY AND STANDARD ACT 2006' - SUPREME COURT AND HIGH COURT's LEADING CASE LAWS

54. ARMED FORCE TRIBUNAL ACT- SUPREME COURT'S LATEST LEADING CASE LAWs

55. ESSENTIAL COMMODITIES ACT 1955- SUPREME COURT'S LATEST LEADING CASE LAWS

56. 'FOREIGN TRADE DEVELOPMENT AND REGULATION ACT'- SUPREME COURT AND HIGH COURT'S LEADING CASE LAWS

57.'PARTNERSHIP ACT 1932'- SUPREME COURT'S LEADING CASE LAWS

58. 'COTPA ACT 2003' - SUPREME COURT AND HIGH COURT'S LEADING CASE LAWS

59. DOMESTIC VIOLENCE ACT 2005' - SUPREME COURT'S LEADING CASE LAWS

60. 'DOWRY PROHIBITION ACT 1961' - SUPREME COURT'S LATEST CASE LAWS

Books are available online in India

1. Notion Press: https://notionpress.com/author/jayprakash_somani

2. Amazon: https://www.amazon.in/s?k=jayprakash+somani

3. Flipkart: https://www.flipkart.com/search?q=Jayprakash%20Somani

Books are available online at International Market

4. Amazon International: https://www.amazon.com/s?k=jayprakash+somani

5. Amazon United Kingdom: https://www.amazon.co.uk/s?k=jayprakash+somani

6. E-Books/Kindle edition at National & International Level: https://www.amazon.in/s?k=jaypraksh+somani

Adv Jayprakash Somani's Online Courses

Download our app to get access to our Free Videos, Free Bare Acts, Free Study Material in Legal as well as International Business Regime.

Android App Link ;-https://clpandrea.page.link/cmSm

Ios APp Link :-https://apps.apple.com/us/app/classplus/id1324522260

Login with org code ;- (qywzji)

Web Link ;-https://qywzji.courses.store/

Download App on Google play store - Type

<u>Jayprakash Somani SupremeCourt</u>

Legal Courses :

1. SLP- Bail Matters- Drafting & Successful Arguing in the Supreme Court.

Description - This Course is helpful to Advocates, Litigants, Law Officers, Law Students, Law Schools, Individual. Course contains 8 Videos + Study Material+ PDF Books. Access to this course is for Two Years. Expected duration of this course is one month only.

Topics : 1. SLP- Bail Matters- Drafting & Successful Arguing in the Supreme Court, **2.** Types of bails, **3.** Laws related to bail matters, **4.** How to read Impugned Order of High Court & frame substantial question of laws, **5.** How to draft excellent SLP, **6.** Searching of citations/ case laws, **7.** How to argue in admission hearings, **8.** How argue in after notice hearing.

Speaker: Jayprakash Bansilal Somani, MBA (Foreign Trade), LL. B. Advocate, Supreme Court of India & IP www.jayprakashsomani.com Call: P. A. 9322188701

2. SLP- Succession Matters- Drafting & Successful Arguing in the Supreme Court.

Description - This Course is helpful to Advocates, Litigants, Law Officers, Law Students, Law Schools, Individual. Course contains 9 Videos + Study Material+ PDF Books. Access to this course is for Two Years. Expected duration of this course is one month only.

Topics :1. SLP- Succession Matters- Drafting & Successful Arguing in the Supreme Court, **2.** Information about Succession Matters, **3.** Laws related to Succession Matters, **4.** How to read Impugned Order of High Court to frame substantial questions of law, **5.** How to draft excellent synopsis & list of date, **6.** Drafting of SLP of Succession Matter, **7.** Searching of citations/ case laws, **8.** How to prepare notes & then argue in admission hearings, **9.** How to prepare notes & then argue in after notice final hearing.

Speaker: Jayprakash Bansilal Somani, MBA (Foreign Trade), LL. B. Advocate, Supreme Court of India & IP www.jayprakashsomani.com Call: P. A. 9322188701

3. Legal Vocabulary & its practice pattern to Argue in High Court and Supreme Court / Improve Your Legal English

Description - This Course is helpful to Advocates, Litigants, Law Officers, Law Students, Law Schools, Individual. Course contains 11 Videos + Study Material+ PDF Books. Access to this course is for Two Years. Expected duration of this course is three month only.

Topics : 1. Legal Vocabulary & its practice pattern to Argue in High Court and Supreme Court / Improve Your Legal English, **2.** 1000 legal verbs with its three forms, **3.** Twelve Tenses with its running practice, **4.** One Pdf book on legal vocabulary & its practice pattern with Latin Terms, **5.** Second Pdf book on legal vocabulary & its practice pattern with Latin Terms, **6.** Some Videos of CJI Dr. Dhananjay Chandrachud for the practice of good legal English, **7.** Some Video/Audio Lectures of Legend Nani Palkhivala for standard perfect legal English & flow of Speech, **8.** Some Videos of renowned Sr. Advocates from Mumbai for flow, legal vocabulary & their struggle in legal journey, **9.** Some Videos of Sr. Advocates of the Supreme Court for flow & legal vocabulary, **10.** Some Videos of foreign persons to improve Professional English & thinking process in English, **11.** Some important legal doctrines with case laws.

Speaker: Jayprakash Bansilal Somani, MBA (Foreign Trade), LL. B. Advocate, Supreme Court of India & IP www.jayprakashsomani.com Call: P. A. 9322188701.

4. SLP- Property Matters - Drafting and Successful Arguing in the Supreme Court.

Description - This Course is helpful to Advocates, Litigants, Law Officers, Law Students, Law Schools 8 Individual. Course contains 9 Videos + Study Material+ PDF Books. Access to this course is for Two Years. Expected duration of this course is one month only.

Topics : 1. SLP- Property Matters - Drafting and Successful Arguing in the Supreme Court, **2.** Types of Property Matters, **3.** Laws related to Property Matters, **4.** How to read Impugned Order of High Court to guide client & frame substantial question of laws, **5.** How to draft Synopsis & List of Dates in Property Matter, **6.** How to draft excellent SLP of Property Matter, **7.** Searching of citations/ case laws with specific paras, **8.** How to argue confidently in admission hearings, **9.** How argue confidently in after notice & final hearings.

Speaker: Jayprakash Bansilal Somani, MBA (Foreign Trade), LL. B. Advocate, Supreme Court of India & IP www.jayprakashsomani.com Call: P. A. 9322188701.

International Business Courses -

1. Agri Products Exports - Scope from India.

Description - This Course is helpful to Agriculturalists, Entrepreneurs, Exporters, Importers, Students. Course contains 12 Videos + Study Material+ PDF Books. Access to this course is for Two Years. Expected duration of this course is one month only.

Topics : **1-** Agri Products Exports - Scope from India, **2.** Agri Export's share in India's total export, **3.** Agri Export Promotional Council's Support, **4.** Top 10 Agri export countries, **5.** Top 10 Agri export product, **6.** India's share in World's Agri Exports, **7.** Onion Exports from India, **8.** Rice Exports from India, **9.** Mango Exports from India, **10.** Fresh Vegetable Exports, **11.** Fresh Fruits Exports, **12.** Export of Agri Allied Products.

Speaker: Jayprakash Bansilal Somani, MBA (Foreign Trade), LL. B. Advocate, Supreme Court of India & IP www.jayprakashsomani.com Call: P. A. 9322188701.

2. Textile Exports - Scope from India.

Description - This Course is helpful to Textile Business Houses, Entrepreneurs, Exporters, Importers, Students. Course contains 14 Videos

+ Study Material+ PDF Books. Access to this course is for Two Years. Expected duration of this course is one month only.

Topics : 1- Textile Exports - Scope from India, 2. Textile Export's share in India's total exports, 3. Support of Textile Export Promotional Council, 4. Top 10 Countries in Textile Exports, 5. Top 10 Products in Textile Exports, 6. Export of Readymade Garments, 7. Export of Man-made Textiles, 8. Export of Handloom Products, 9. Export of Wool & Woollen Textiles, 10. Export of Silk, 11. Exports of Handicrafts & Carpets, 12. Exports of Coir & Coir Manufacturers, 13. Exports of Jute,14. India's share in World's total textile expor.

Speaker: Jayprakash Bansilal Somani, MBA (Foreign Trade), LL. B. Advocate, Supreme Court of India & IP www.jayprakashsomani.com Call: P. A. 9322188701.

3. Export Import Procedure -Perfect Documentation & It's Management.

Description -This Course is helpful to Business Men, Service Providers, Entrepreneurs, Exporters, Importers, Students. Course contains 13 Videos + Study Material+ PDF Books. Access to this course is for Two Years. Expected duration of this course is three months only.

Topics : 1. Export Import Procedure, Perfect Documentation & Its management, 2. Company Formation, 3. Opening of Bank Account in AD Bank, 4. Export Procedure points, 5. Import Procedure Points, 6. Taking Import Export Code, 7. Taking RCMC number, 8. Registration at Port when necessary, 9. Quality Inspection Certificate of Goods, 10. CHA & its roll, 11. Custom Formalities, 12. Export Documents such as Invoice, Bill of Lading, Insurance Certificate, Quality Inspection Certificate & others, 13. Excellent Management of Export & Imports Documents.

Speaker: Jayprakash Bansilal Somani, MBA (Foreign Trade), LL. B. Advocate, Supreme Court of India & IP www.jayprakashsomani.com Call: P. A. 9322188701.

4. Jewellery Exports -Scope from India

Description - You can understand world wide scope for Jems & Jewellery in multidimensional ways. 14 videos of this course will create positive spark among you to enter into the Exports & Imports of Gems & Jewellery and other products. Chance to ask your query to Somani Sir every week.

Topics :1. Jewellery Exports - Scope from India, 2. Jewellery Export's share in India's total exports, 3. Support of Jems & Jewellery Export

Promotional Council, **4.** Top 10 Countries in Jewellery Exports, **5.** Top 10 Products in Jewellery Exports, **6.** Export of Cut & Polished Diamonds, **7.** Export of Gold Jewellery, **8.** Export of Plain Gold Jewellery, **9.** Export of Studded Gold Jewellery, **10.** Export of Silver Jewellery, **11.** Exports of Platinum Jewellery, **12.** Exports of Imitation Jewellery, **13.** Exports of Articles of Gold, Silver & others, **14.** India's share in World's total Jewellery export.

Speaker: Jayprakash Bansilal Somani, MBA (Foreign Trade), LL. B. Advocate, Supreme Court of India & IP www.jayprakashsomani.com Call: P. A. 9322188701.

5. Export Import Finance Management with LC, ECGC & Venture Capital.

Description -You can understand A to Z about International Finance with LC, ECGC & Venture Capital in simple language & with illustrations. 11 videos of this course will create positive spark among you regarding International Finance Management with practical tips. Chance to ask your query to Somani Sir every week.

Topics : **1.** Export Import Finance Management with LC, ECGC & Venture Capital, **2.** Which is good & excellent source of finance, **3.** Banking Finance, **4.** List of Banks which provides finance for International Business, **5.** How to start business in Less or Zero Capital, **6.** Letter of Credit, **7.** Types of LCs **8.** Scrutiny of L/C, **9.** ECGC Policy, **10.** Venture Capital Finance., **11.** Ideal formula of Investment & continues growth.

Speaker: Jayprakash Bansilal Somani, MBA (Foreign Trade), LL. B. Advocate, Supreme Court of India & IP www.jayprakashsomani.com Call: P. A. 9322188701.

6. Shipping & Logistics in International Business with live links of Ports, ICDs, CHAs etc.

Description - This Course is helpful to any Businessman, Professionals, Entrepreneurs, Exporters, Importers, CHAs, & Students.

Course contains following 10 Videos + Study Material+ PDF Books. Access to this course is for Two Years. Expected duration of this course is three months only.

Topics : **1.** Shipping & Logistics in International Business with live links of Ports, ICDs, CHAs etc, **2.** Roll of CHA in Shipping & Logistics of International Business, **3.** How to find good & genuine CHA, **4.** Courier/ post service for small parcel, **5.** India's important Ports & ICDs with live links, **6.** How & what to study Ports/ ICDs websites, **7.** Art to reduce charges of Shipping & logistics, **8.** Information about some Top International Ports with live links, **9.** Roll of Customs in Exports & Imports,**10.** How to become CHA .

Speaker: Jayprakash Bansilal Somani, MBA (Foreign Trade), LL. B. Advocate, Supreme Court of India & IP www.jayprakashsomani.com Call: P. A. 9322188701.

7. International Business Marketing Part 1: Finding Potential & Genuine Buyers for Exports and Suppliers for Imports.

Description -You can understand Seven Excellent ways to Find Potential & Genuine Buyers for Exports and Suppliers for Imports with illustrations. 11 videos of this course will create positive spark among you regarding International Business Marketing with practical tips. Chance to ask your query to Somani Sir every week.

Topics : 1. International Business Marketing Part 1: Finding Potential & Genuine Buyers for Exports and Suppliers for Imports,**2.** Seven Excellent Ways to find Potential Buyers for Exports, **3.** Top 20 B to B Websites in the World, **4.** Searching Potential Buyers from B to B Sites. Is this safe & good way to search potential buyers, **5.** Searching Potential Buyers through Export Promotional Councils & Its Magazines, **6.** Searching Potential Buyers with help from Embassies, **7.** Searching Potential Buyers through Chamber of Commerce at global level, **8.** Searching Potential Buyers from International Trade Fairs & Exhibitions, **9.** Searching Potential Buyers through your friends & relatives or any Indian Person in focus countries, **10.** How to find focus countries for your products or services, **11.** Taking references from establish buyer/seller.

Speaker: Jayprakash Bansilal Somani, MBA (Foreign Trade), LL. B. Advocate, Supreme Court of India & IP www.jayprakashsomani.com Call: P. A. 9322188701.

8. International Business Marketing Part 2: Communication Skill to take repeated orders from Potential Buyers

Description - You can learn Perfect Communication Skills to initiate International Trade with foreign buyers and art to take repeated orders from these Potential Buyers with illustrations. 11 videos of this course will create positive spark among you to reach upto One Star Exporter Level rapidly and subsequent journey to reach upto Five Star Export House. Chance to ask your query to Somani Sir every week.

Topics :1. International Business Marketing Part 2: Communication Skill to take repeated orders from Potential Buyers,**2.** Preparation of

Impressive Company Profile, **3.** Excellent Product CatLog for International Market, **4.** Phone Calls with maintaining dignity of ourself & our country, **5.** Sending emails, **6.** Sending what's app messages, **7.** Technique of repeated follow up, **8.** Art of taking 100% advance payments, **9.** Before giving credit facility how to look credibility of potential buyers or suppliers, **10.** Art of earning good profit of margin, **11.** Art of managing international clients.

Speaker: Jayprakash Bansilal Somani, MBA (Foreign Trade), LL. B. Advocate, Supreme Court of India & IP www.jayprakashsomani.com Call: P. A. 9322188701.